Hammurabi

A Captivating Guide to the Sixth King of the First Babylonian Dynasty, Including the Code of Hammurabi

© **Copyright 2018**

All Rights Reserved. No part of this book may be reproduced in any form without permission in writing from the author. Reviewers may quote brief passages in reviews.

Disclaimer: No part of this publication may be reproduced or transmitted in any form or by any means, mechanical or electronic, including photocopying or recording, or by any information storage and retrieval system, or transmitted by email without permission in writing from the publisher.

While all attempts have been made to verify the information provided in this publication, neither the author nor the publisher assumes any responsibility for errors, omissions or contrary interpretations of the subject matter herein.

This book is for entertainment purposes only. The views expressed are those of the author alone, and should not be taken as expert instruction or commands. The reader is responsible for his or her own actions.

Adherence to all applicable laws and regulations, including international, federal, state and local laws governing professional licensing, business practices, advertising and all other aspects of doing business in the US, Canada, UK or any other jurisdiction is the sole responsibility of the purchaser or reader.

Neither the author nor the publisher assumes any responsibility or liability whatsoever on the behalf of the purchaser or reader of these materials. Any perceived slight of any individual or organization is purely unintentional.

Free Bonus from Captivating History (Available for a Limited time)

Hi History Lovers!

Now you have a chance to join our exclusive history list so you can get your first history ebook for free as well as discounts and a potential to get more history books for free! Simply visit the link below to join.

Captivatinghistory.com/ebook

Also, make sure to follow us on:

Twitter: @Captivhistory

Facebook: Captivating History:@captivatinghistory

Contents

INTRODUCTION 1

CHAPTER 1 – BABYLON BEFORE HAMMURABI: POSITION OF THE CITY IN MESOPOTAMIA, EARLY RULERS 3

    POSITION OF BABYLON - GEOGRAPHY 3

    POSITION OF BABYLON – POLITICS AND POWER 4

    EARLY RULERS OF BABYLON 5

CHAPTER 2 – RISE OF HAMMURABI: WARS AND ACHIEVEMENTS ..7

    CHRONOLOGY OF HAMMURABI 7

    EARLY YEARS 8

    BEATING ELAM 12

    ATTACKING, SACKING, AND CONQUERING LARSA 17

    THE DEFEAT OF ESHNUNNA 21

    NORTHERN KINGDOMS AND HAMMURABI 25

    MARI'S SUBMISSION 29

CHAPTER 3 – REIGN OF HAMMURABI: BABYLON DURING HIS REIGN, RELATIONS TO OTHER CITIES 34

    HAMMURABI'S BABYLON 34

    Babylon and Other Cities 37
CHAPTER 4 – HAMMURABI'S CHARACTER: PHYSICAL APPEARANCE, RELATIONS WITH OTHER RULERS, GLIMPSES OF HIS PERSONALITY **39**
    What Did Hammurabi Look Like? 39
    Hammurabi's Personality – Dealing with Others 41
CHAPTER 5 – THE CODE OF HAMMURABI AND EARLY MESOPOTAMIAN LAW **44**
    Discovery of the Code 44
    The Appearance of the Stele 45
    The Composition of the Code 46
    Social Stratification of Babylonians..47
CHAPTER 6: DISSECTING THE CODE **49**
    The Prologue 49
    The Code Proper 51
    The Epilogue 82
    Notes on the Code; Common Misconceptions 84
CHAPTER 7 – HAMMURABI'S LEGACY **86**
CONCLUSION **89**
BIBLIOGRAPHY **96**
NOTES ON IMAGES..**99**

Introduction

Ancient Mesopotamia is a region both shrouded in mystery and laden with fascinating stories. More often than not, they speak of strong heroes, epic rulers, and the matters of both gods and men. And the more we uncover about its history, the more fascinating it becomes. We learn that these people weren't as savage or barbaric as we are today, that their worldviews, attitudes, and everyday customs match ours more closely than once thought, and that they have plenty of stories to tell that are eerily similar to ours.

It's this very region that gave the world some of the most powerful, most enigmatic rulers. Gilgamesh, a king himself, outgrew that title and became a literary, deified figure to many generations to come. Sargon the Great became the first emperor to unite multiple people under his firm hand. Ur-Nammu rekindled the Sumerian old ways and gave the region one of the most developed, exalted cultures to exist in the ancient Middle East. And these are merely three of the dozens of rulers that, in one way or another, changed the world set between the Tigris and the Euphrates.

However, there are very few, if any, kings of this region as revered, as mighty, and as famed as the Babylonian king known as Hammurabi. Reading the endless barrage of literature about this monarch gives us a vivid picture of how a tiny, insignificant city became the dominant force in the Middle East, how a marginal ruler became the great unifier who brought about the laws of the land and pacified vast peoples of many different cities, and how the area between the two great rivers became united for the first time, even if it lasted less than half a decade.

Reading on, you will learn of who Hammurabi actually was. You'll see where Babylon stood during the rule of his immediate ancestors, what Hammurabi did before he decided to wage war against the world, how others saw him—from rival rulers to his own dignitaries—and how his now-famous Code came to prominence. You'll also learn more about this very Code, what it was (and what it wasn't), what it contained (and what it no longer contains), how it was lost, how it was found, and how its discovery brought Hammurabi back into the public eye many millennia later.

The story of Hammurabi is the story of forty-three years jampacked with conquest, temple and wall building, irrigation efforts, and lawmaking, but it's also a story of broken relations and rising and falling empires. It's a story of betrayal and shifting alliances, a story where even the gods take a backseat to the matters of common men. It's a tale that's both thousands of years old and, interestingly enough, just as contemporary as it was when Hammurabi still drew breath. And, like all great tales of history, it's a yarn that teaches the common man that no feat of greatness comes without a price, and that human nature is just as complex as it was when Babylonians praised Marduk and hailed Hammurabi as a god in his own right.

Chapter 1 – Babylon Before Hammurabi: Position of the City in Mesopotamia, Early Rulers

It's not an exaggeration to say that Babylon became a prominent and important city because of Hammurabi. Before this king came to power, the city was little more than a vassal state to other major powers at the time. In fact, when one takes into account that Hammurabi was the sixth ruler of the First Babylonian dynasty and that literally no ruler before him has any noteworthy mention in the contemporary Babylonian texts (other than the usual year dates and an occasional cuneiform letter here or there), you can see how instrumental this king was to the rapid development of this city. In this respect, Babylon is much like Akkad and Isin before it, and both Sargon the Great and Ishbi-Erra, to an extent, stand shoulder to shoulder with Hammurabi in terms of putting their respective cities "on the map," so to speak.

Position of Babylon - Geography

Babylon was located in today's Hillah within the Babil governorate in Iraq. In terms of ancient Mesopotamia, the city was closest to ancient Kish, south of Sippar and Eshnunna and north of Nippur and Isin. Despite how minor it was in terms of power and politics, Babylon was still an important river port, as the Euphrates went right through the city, "splitting" it in two. Part of the reason why a lot of Babylon remains unexcavated is because the river eventually changed course, and a section of the city wound up under water.

The archeological site of Babylon today consists of several mounds. Each of these mounds stretches in an area roughly 2 by 1 km or 1.2 by 0.6 miles in size and they contain mud bricks and debris. Like all Mesopotamian cities, Babylon had no major forests nor was there a major mountain in its close vicinity. As such, it had issues obtaining raw materials such as wood, stone, different metals, and precious stones, but it had an abundance of fish, different crops, and cattle. Of course, Babylon relied on trade and had a well-developed network of river-faring merchants.

Position of Babylon – Politics and Power

The first mention of Babylon as a city comes to us from the time of Sargon of Akkad, as he boasted that he had rebuilt temples in this town. At the time, Babylon had no significant rulers and merely existed as a port along the Euphrates. There was a debate within the scholar community about Sargon being the original founder of Babylon, which is largely accepted as apocryphal. A few historians even attribute the founding of Babylon to a later Assyrian ruler known as Sargon II. However, the original Sargon's dynasty did indeed have their fingerprints over this, at the time, tiny city.

Naram-sin, the legendary ruler almost as revered as his ancestor Sargon (and who ruled a quarter of a century after him), held most of Mesopotamia in his grasp and even declared himself a god during his lifetime. However, maintaining an empire of this size only brought problems to his son and successor, Shar-kali-sharri. Considering how many defensive wars this emperor had to participate in, it was only natural that he had to maintain order in non-Akkadian territories his father conquered, and that meant appeasing the constituents. In ancient Mesopotamia at the time, this meant repairing and rebuilding old temples and building new ones. One of the cities where Shar-kali-sharri built a new temple was

Nippur, an important religious and political city of the entire region. Curiously, the second city that Shar-kali-sharri honored with a new temple, or rather two temples (which we have available records of), was Babylon. While this action in and of itself didn't elevate Babylon to a position of higher influence, it was still a noteworthy event that, we can assume, tells us the city held at least some prominence to an ancient Mesopotamian man.

The famous Ur III period didn't "ignore" Babylon either. Throughout the reign of Ur's last five Sumerian rulers, Babylon had to pay in-kind taxes, i.e., taxes in goods rather than money. In addition, the kings of Ur appointed local governors themselves, letting us know that Babylon was indeed subordinate to them in full.

Early Rulers of Babylon

After the fall of Ur, the entire area where Babylon lay was conquered by Amorites. While they were Semitic themselves, they spoke with a different dialect and had an entirely different lifestyle to the Semitic people inhabiting cities. Like most tribes outside of Mesopotamia proper, they were nomadic and rarely settled. However, with the passage of time, some of the Amorite merchants actually established strong dynasties of many independent cities, and their influence kept growing.

Babylon at the time was a vassal state of Kazallu. Sources vary, but the first ruler to break Babylon away from Kazallu was one Sumu-Abum, also known as Su-abu. Alongside his son, Sumu-la-El, he's regarded as the builder of Babylon's walls, and it's still debatable which one is the proper "first" ruler of Babylon.

This problem of "picking" the first ruler of Babylon actually continues up to Hammurabi's father and predecessor, Sin-Muballit. The four rulers before him—Sumu-Abum, Sumu-la-El, Sabium, and Apil-Sin—were all kings, but neither of the four claimed kingship of the city itself. In other words, the center of their kingdom, whatever it was, wasn't Babylon. Sin-Muballit was the first ruler to break away from this practice and use that title in reference to the city.

Of course, Sin-Muballit didn't differ from his predecessors in this respect alone. In fact, this pre-Hammurabi king is the one we have the most available data of. Unlike the four kings before him, Sin-Muballit actually expanded the territory of the city, and in a remarkable way. Namely, he took control of Isin, which was a major powerhouse itself not long before. Granted, by the time of Sin-Muballit, Isin was a shell of its former self, which made it easy to conquer, but in terms of military successes, this was still a major one for a ruler of an insignificant city such as Babylon was at the time. Before the end of his reign, Babylon held dominion over Borsippa, Sippar, and Kish.

One look at the year names, or calendar dates, of Sin-Muballit tells us of his prolific tradition of building temples and rebuilding and fortifying walls. Much like any conqueror before him, Sin-Muballit was likely trying to win favor with his subjects, and major construction projects were the typical way to do this. He is also credited, again via year names, of digging and maintaining a few canals. Before we move on, we ought to stress that, at the time, all Ancient Mesopotamian monarchs "named" their years after a particular achievement or important event. Much like all contemporary sources, they aren't entirely reliable, as they were often used to boost the ruler's position and at times outright ignored contemporary historical facts.

Despite his conquests, however, it's likely that he was himself a vassal, or at least a subordinate, of Shamshi-Adad I. As such, he was the contemporary of the expansion of Larsa under Rim-Sin I, the sack of Isin by said ruler, and the growth and expansion of Eshnunna, Elam, and Mari, all of them at some point both allies and enemies of his son. It is widely accepted that he abdicated the throne due to failing health.

Chapter 2 – Rise of Hammurabi: Wars and Achievements

Chronology of Hammurabi

Before we move onto what Hammurabi did and when he did it, it's important to talk about chronologies, as they are intimately related to this ruler.

Two widely accepted ways of dating events in early history are called the short and the middle chronology (though they are by no means the only ones). The discrepancy between the two roughly equates 64 years. For this particular topic, we shall be using the middle chronology since it's a bit more accurate than the short one, though still not as reliable as historians would want it to be.

Another stumbling block is the fact that the Babylonian year was based on the lunar calendar and began in March rather than January. This means that, at times, the Babylonian years lasted 13 months rather than 12. Despite using the term "BCE" here, you should take these particularities into consideration, as these dates don't really coincide perfectly with the Common Era dates we use today.

Early Years

Most major events during Hammurabi's reign occur after 1792 BCE when he took over the throne from his father. When it comes to their origins, the entire family tree of Hammurabi has Amorite origins. Naturally, it's difficult to distinguish between native Semitic tribes at the time, and while names can be an indicator of the origins of a person in Mesopotamia, oftentimes it can further complicate things. Sin-Muballit, for example, translates to "the god Sin (Nanna) is the giver of life," and every word of that name is Akkadian rather than Amorite. But Hammurabi's name is a compound of both an Amorite term and an Akkadian adjective. "Hammu" or even "Ammu" means "family," and it's an Amorite term. "Rabi" or "Rapi," on the other hand, is Akkadian and means "great, grand." So, the rough meaning of his name is "a kinsman who heals," or even "an uncle is a healer."

The year 1792 is taken as his first year in power in the middle chronology. He ruled a grand total of 43 years, and we have year names of almost all of them, though some, of course, are damaged and difficult to discern. That's why it's difficult to place the creation of Hammurabi's famous Code, though the consensus usually puts it somewhere in the final four or five years of Hammurabi's reign, based on the Code's prologue. We shall discuss this in the chapter dedicated to the Code, and for now we'll focus on the first ten or so years of this great king's long reign.

Around this time, major kingdoms of old were either falling apart or already part of history. Isin, already once sacked by Hammurabi's father, also suffered under the mighty Rim-Sin of Larsa. Rim-Sin was still a contemporary of Hammurabi and, if the chronology is to be believed, was already in his mid- to late sixties when the young Babylonian sat on the throne. Larsa was a force in and of itself, developing somewhat parallel to Isin after the fall of Ur centuries ago. Rim-Sin and Sin-Muballit were foes in the last decade of the 18th century BCE, and one of their skirmishes involved Isin and Uruk, where a coalition of monarchs (including Sin-Muballit) revolted against the king of Larsa. These revolts were not without reason; Rim-Sin was growing more powerful, uniting most of southern Mesopotamia and, apparently, not slowing down. Controlling the riverways, either in the north or the south, was the goal of any ruler, as these were the most lucrative aspects of these regions. Not only were they great sources of fish and arable land, but they were also like "highways" of the region, as it was where everything was transported—cattle, grain, people, statues, you name it. Any ruler who was close to capturing these riverways was a threat, and threats like these would result in common, yet always shaky, partnerships.

But Rim-Sin wasn't the only powerful ruler of the region. Shamshi-Adad, another Amorite like Hammurabi, ruled a vast area known by its modern moniker "Upper Mesopotamia." His greatest achievement is the conquest of Assur, making him, technically, an Assyrian king. He legitimized himself as one by adding his name to the official king's list of Assur, a practice which ended with his successor, Ishme-Dagan. Prior to the conquest of the Assyrian capital, however, Shamshi-Adad took over a city on the Tigris River called Ekallatum, as well as a few other settlements originally under Eshnunna, another powerful city-state at the time. What Rim-Sin was in the south, Shamshi-Adad was in the north—a capable conqueror with aspirations for more territory and a long list of enemies.

Mari, to the northwest of Babylon and southwest of Assur, was another major player in the region. Shamshi-Adad took it over in 1796, four years before Hammurabi ascended to the throne. He had appointed his son, Yasmah-Adad, as the ruler of the city, whereas Ishme-Dagan ruled Ekallatum. According to the correspondences at the time, Shamshi-Adad wasn't pleased with his son, and after his death, that same son of his would be defeated by a new ruler native to Mari called Zimri-Lim. This descendant of the Lim dynasty would be a major player during Hammurabi's reign, both as an ally and as an enemy to the Babylonian king.

However, Zimri-Lim wasn't the only ruler of this region to have communicated with Hammurabi. In fact, Yasmah-Adad wrote directly to the king, not treating him entirely favorably. As a still minor ruler with a small territory (which, aside from Babylon, included Kish, Sippar, and Borsippa), Hammurabi was more than likely treated as a mere vassal by both Shamshi-Adad and his sons during his earliest years on the throne.

Two additional powers also held dominion over others during the early years of Hammurabi. One was in the deep south, the Elamite state, with Susa as its capital. Rulers of Elam had influence as far north as Babylon, and their kingdom was strong, with a massive army and a long history of successful warfare. However, they didn't really do much during Hammurabi's first years, opting to stay on the sidelines. The second power that claimed the fertile Mesopotamian lands was Eshnunna. While they, like Elam, didn't go after Babylon directly during the time of the First Dynasty, they still maintained a powerful stranglehold of several key areas around the Tigris, a few of which were found around modern Baghdad.

The stage was then set—Shamshi-Adad's state was beginning to crumble, Rim-Sin was still working on expanding Larsa's influence, Elam and Eshnunna remained on the sidelines (yet not entirely so), and Mari was undergoing a tumultuous rebirth. Where did this period see Hammurabi, though?

The first decade of Hammurabi's reign didn't contain a lot of wars. The most notable ones were campaigns against Uruk and Isin, as well as a campaign against a still unidentified city of Malgium. This city was evidently already under Elamite rule, but then Hammurabi "liberated it" by way of conquest. Still, these weren't particularly important events during this decade, at least not as important as Hammurabi's "establishing of justice throughout the land" and his building of a massive canal called "Hammurabi is abundance." Much like numerous rulers before him, Hammurabi wanted to earn favor with his subjects, and he did so by annulling or paying for outstanding debts. What followed was a series of temple and wall building campaigns, both in Babylon and in other occupied territories. Irrigation remained an important factor in a city's survival, so his choice to build and maintain a massive canal is hardly revolutionary. Aside from this, he also rebuilt and repaired a pre-existing canal dug by his grandfather Apil-Sin.

Hammurabi's second decade was equally lacking in terms of military conquest, as was his third. Two cities, Rapiqum and Szalibi, fell under his control soon after his conquest of Malgium. However, for the following nineteen years, according to the official year names, he didn't start any military campaigns. Most of this time was devoted to building temples, creating statues of various deities, and rebuilding cities in his possession. Most of these statues were made in honor of the sun god Shamash (Utu, in Sumerian), despite the fact that Babylon had a different titular deity, a still minor god called Marduk. It's hard to know what he was originally the god of, but most people associate him with water, judgment, vegetation, and magic. Naturally, after Hammurabi, the cult of Marduk grew, and he gained a wider following, which speaks volumes of this king's influence over the region. In fact, Hammurabi himself was deified, which we will touch upon in later chapters.

One particular statue Hammurabi devoted an entire year to was that of Ishtar, or Inanna, the goddess of fertility, sex, and love, among other things. Even before Hammurabi, the cult of Inanna was widespread among rulers, and she was almost as important as Enlil, the god of the winds, or Anu, the ancestor of all Mesopotamian gods. Kings would regularly call themselves "consorts of Inanna" and perform rituals where they would marry the goddess. Semitic people (Akkadians and Babylonians included) had a largely similar religious system to the older Sumerians, and Hammurabi merely followed in the footsteps of his own ancestors when it came to this matter.

It wasn't until the 30th year of his rule that Hammurabi became the conqueror he's remembered as.

Beating Elam

Elam was farther south than the other states, bordering the highlands of what is Fars today. The mountains at its edge contained precious raw materials such as tin and lapis lazuli. The former was often used to create bronze, which would further be fashioned into weaponry such as axes and blades. Lapis lazuli, on the other hand, was a commodity due to its beautiful blue color. Early Sumerians used it for creating jewelry, statues, and other trinkets of high value. Not only did Elam have direct access to these goods, but they also controlled all trade routes to get them. In short, Elam held economic sway over its northern and western Mesopotamian neighbors.

As stated earlier, Elam didn't go after the Mesopotamian states during the early years of Hammurabi's reign. They would occasionally help out a ruler here or there, such as when Shamshi-Adad led a campaign against the mountain-folk of Zagros in 1781 BCE, but other than that they didn't really interfere in Mesopotamia's complicated politics. However, events that followed slowly changed the minds of Elamites, and they shifted from a somewhat passive observer to an active warring conqueror.

Shamshi-Adad died in 1776, which resulted in an expected fragmentation and decline of his massive state. His sons were still in power, but more and more rebellions popped up everywhere. However, the problem his dying empire was facing had more to do with external rather than internal politics. In other words, the declining empire centered around Assur was facing the rise of other city-states, with Eshnunna being a major player. Eshnunna was an important port city of the Tigris River, but more importantly, it stood between Elam and the passage to the other great river, the Euphrates. Nine years after Shamshi-Adad's death, in 1767, Elam's ruler, Siwe-Palar-Khuppak, began his correspondence with Zimri-Lim of Mari, who at the time had taken full control of the city, liberating it from Yasmah-Adad and possibly even killing him. Zimri-Lim did this with the aid of Yarim-Lim, the second ruler of Yamhad; this kingdom had then established seniority over Mari and would be an important ally of Hammurabi after the events of the 1767 conflict between Mari and Elam.

But before they became enemies, Mari and Elam were allies. Zimri-Lim wanted to crush the king of Eshnunna, Ibal-pi-el II, since he led regular raids and attacks on Mari territory. Babylon was also part of this alliance, but without any direct warring on the side of Hammurabi. Sometime between the end of 1766 and the beginning of 1765, Elam and its allies sacked Eshnunna, and Ibal-pi-el II was nowhere to be seen, likely dying in the conflict. Siwe-Palar-Khuppak thus became an overlord of Eshnunna, and at that point, Elam had an important piece of territory that cut deep within Mesopotamia.

But the king of Elam was insatiable. Treating Zimri-Lim and Hammurabi as subordinate serfs, he ordered them to send him troops for a potential invasion of Larsa. Let's not forget, Larsa was still ruled by a very much alive, very active, and very war-hungry Rim-Sin I—in other words, a ruler not to be trifled with. Yet Siwe-Palar-Khuppak contacted him as well, proposing a potential sack of Babylon. Both Mari and Babylon learned of this, but despite Elam's duplicitous political behavior, Mari remained loyal. That loyalty would, however, slowly wane in time.

Babylon would prove instrumental in the crush of Elam in more ways than one. Siwe-Palar-Khuppak actually coveted Babylon for a very long time and constantly pressured Zimri-Lim to assist him in conquering it. At the same time, Hammurabi kept sending gifts and maintained a lively correspondence with the king of Mari, urging him to raise an army and help him defeat the Elamites. With some difficulty, Zimri-Lim managed to gather a sizable army of roughly 2,000 people led by two generals: Zimri-Addu and Ibal-pi-el (not to be confused with the king of Eshnunna; interestingly, that king, deposed by Zimri-Lim, was once an ally of Hammurabi and actively waged wars against Shamshi-Adad in order to crush his kingdom).

But even the combined armies of Babylon and Mari weren't enough to drive the Elamites away. Hammurabi then turned to the state of Yamhad and its own ruler, who had proven to be an ally of Mari having helped establish Zimri-Lim on his throne. At the time, Yamhad was ruled, interestingly, by its own Hammurabi, or to be more precise, Hammurabi I, son of Yarim-Lim. Interesting factoids don't end there, however; Yamhad, unlike Babylon, had no less than three rulers named Hammurabi, with the first being a contemporary of his Babylonian namesake. While he was getting Yamhad's help, Zimri-Lim contacted the country of Zalmaqum, which, in turn, sent some of its own troops to be led by the king of Mari rather than Hammurabi.

The Babylonian king continued rallying troops. The next ruler he contacted was none other than Ishme-Dagan, the son of the late Shamshi-Adad. Interestingly, the roles of the rulers of these two countries, Babylon and Upper Mesopotamia respectively, shifted with the death of Shamshi-Adad. While he was alive, Hammurabi was his underling in a sense. Shamshi-Adad's son, however, ruled Ekallatum as almost a vassal of the Babylonian monarch. He sent his regiment of men to Hammurabi as a means of defeating Elam but did not do so all too willingly.

Interestingly, Larsa did not get involved in this war. Whatever the reasons behind this were, Rim-Sin joined no side, and now it was down to Elam and its vast land on one side, and a Hammurabi-led coalition of Babylon, Mari, Ekallatum, Yamhad, and Zalmaqum on the other.

Elam attacked first, taking a decisive victory at the city of Upi, where Hammurabi's forces apparently retreated. This occurred in 1765, and the very next year the Elamites went after Mankisum, another city on the Tigris with an important strategic position. The coalition army moved to a small border town called Namsum, unaware where the enemy would strike next.

The city of Hiritum turned out to be the next target of the Elamite king, as it lay close to Babylon-owned Sippar, and the conquest of this city would place the Elamite troops dangerously close to Hammurabi's capital. However, not only did the citizens of Hiritum defend themselves successfully against the invaders (with some help from Mari and Babylonian troops), but the coalition army managed to plunder and raid the Elam-owned territory of Eshnunna as well. Eshnunna, as it turned out, would prove itself to be a sore spot of Elam, as there's evidence of an internal struggle—Eshnunna locals were not entirely prepared to fight in the name of Elam's king. Some of them even went so far as to inquire Hammurabi for his direct help, swearing fealty to him. This city was by no means alone in its betrayal of Elam. A certain ruler named Atamrum decided to abandon Siwe-Palar-Khuppak and ally himself with Zimri-Lim. The Elamites began their retreat, sacking the city of Kakkulatum and moving to the city of Mankisum. This city was exceptionally close to Ishme-Dagan's city-state of Ekallatum, and conquering or even sacking it would deal a significant blow to the coalition. However, Mankisum would be the Elamite king's last advance, considering he had to turn his attention to Eshnunna, which erupted in a full-blown revolt. What began as a small throng of deserters now became an ersatz war of independence, which saw the rise of a local commoner into a ruler. This man was Silli-Sin and, much like Sargon, is one of only a handful of examples Mesopotamia has to offer of non-noble men rising to power.

Silli-Sin was partially responsible for the utter defeat of Siwe-Palar-Khuppak. The king of Elam withdrew to the city of Diniktum and, realizing that he was beaten, sought peace from Hammurabi, a de facto leader of the coalition. Hammurabi showed goodwill at first, releasing the Elamite "ambassadors" which he had imprisoned within Babylon when the war started. However, the king of Elam again began to conspire against the Babylonian ruler by contacting Rim-Sin and Silli-Sin, asking them to form a coalition and sack Babylon. Illness, however, prevented Siwe-Palar-Khuppak from pressing these matters further, and he retreated to Elam to spend the rest of his days.

His retreat was in 1763 BCE, but it was the year prior, 1764, that Hammurabi proclaimed victory over all of Elam, naming the year in honor of the event. It's important to note that the crushing of Elam, the first major victory in his military career, was first and foremost a defensive war, and that it was more of an example of Hammurabi's diplomatic skills and a great deal of luck. The rebellion of Eshnunna and desertion of Atamrum were important pieces of this campaign, and had they not happened, Hammurabi might not have won as decisively, or even won at all. Having armies from four separate rulers—Zimri-Lim, Hammurabi I, Ishme-Dagan, and the unknown king of Zalmaqum—also helped a great deal, considering that Hammurabi's army simply wasn't enough to withstand the invasion of Elam.

Yet, even this war showed that Hammurabi wasn't a perfect diplomat. After all, he didn't secure the help of Rim-Sin, arguably an equal in power to Siwe-Palar-Khuppak, if not even more powerful. This fact alone was enough of a reason for Hammurabi to turn his weapons against Larsa, and with Elam officially out of the picture when it came to the political matters of Mesopotamia, nothing was there to stop him from doing so.

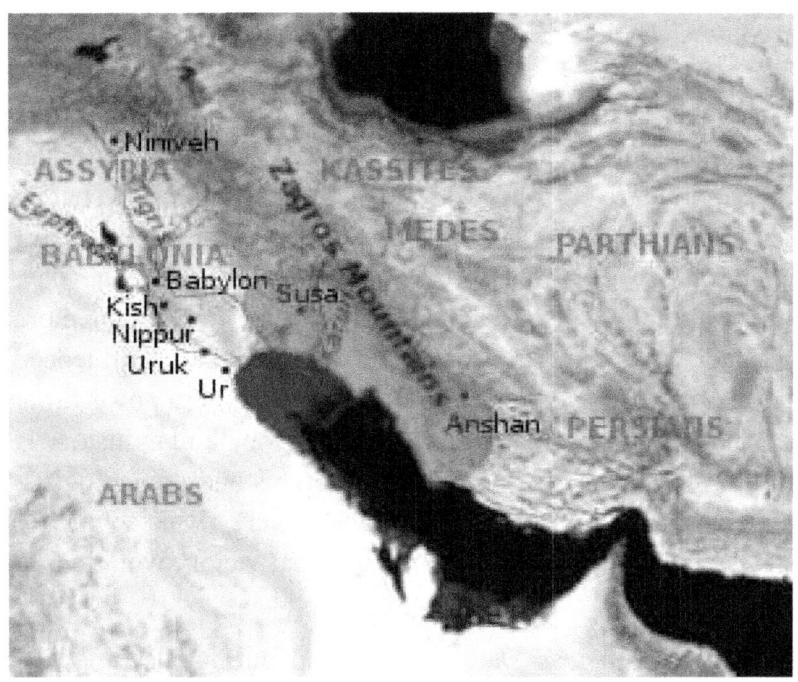

Map of ancient Elam at the height of its power, with other important cities of the region[i]

Attacking, Sacking, and Conquering Larsa

Rim-Sin of Larsa was wise not to interfere in the war against Elam. After all, he had no real reason to go against any of the warring sides. Outright hostile action on Elam would leave his country vulnerable to anyone who wanted to attack him, and going against any of the coalition members would leave him open for Elam to plunder.

During Rim-Sin's time, Larsa reached its military peak. His brother, Warad-Sin, ruled Larsa until 1822 BCE, whereas their father, an Elamite named Kudur-Mabuk held dominion over the country called Yamutbal, with its capital city being Mashkan-shapir. If one takes note of the year, 1822, the conclusion arises that Rim-Sin had died a very old ruler, having dominion over Larsa that lasted a little over 60 years.

Rim-Sin was a warrior; he led campaigns against Isin, Uruk, and Babylon as early as the first decade of his rule. His most important victory, however, was the sack of Isin in 1794 BCE, two years before Hammurabi assumed the throne. The reason this particular victory is important to Rim-Sin was the history the two cities shared. Isin was a kind of "successor state" of the fallen Ur, though it didn't hold dominion over as many cities as Ur did in its heyday. Somehow, parallel to Isin, Larsa was slowly becoming more powerful, and the south of Mesopotamia was politically influenced by either one of these two, depending on who was more powerful at the time. That's why that particular part of Mesopotamian history is usually called the Isin-Larsa period by historians and archeologists. For all intents and purposes, Isin and Larsa were rivals vying for supremacy of the region, and with Rim-Sin, that victory would go to Larsa, albeit shortly.

The last ruler of Isin was Damiq-ilishu, and during his time, the city's territory and influence were reduced to its own walls. Even Hammurabi's father sacked the city years before Rim-Sin's decisive victory. However, it was Rim-Sin's win that echoed in the ancient world, considering he subjugated his major rival and elevated Larsa to the same level Shamshi-Adad's kingdom was at. Babylon and Larsa now shared a long, shaky border, and when Hammurabi took power, Rim-Sin had been established as a capable monarch.

In 1763 BCE, a year after Hammurabi's coalition won their war against Elam, the first sparks of hostility flew between Babylon and Larsa. Hammurabi tried repeatedly to enlist Rim-Sin's help against Elam, but the ruler of Larsa never did so. In fact, he would write to the Babylonian king that his armies were at his disposal, despite no armies being dispatched. Fighting Elam was a difficult campaign, and Hammurabi did not forget Rim-Sin's lack of assistance.

With Elam out of the way, turmoil ensued, as there was no longer a higher power meddling in the affairs of the Mesopotamian kingdoms. But considering how soon armies began advancing against each other (it was probably in early 1763 that Hammurabi declared war on Rim-Sin) and the fact that the same generals, Zimri-Addu and Ibal-pi-el, were commanding Hammurabi's Mari native regiment, it's safe to say that the wars never really stopped, and that the invasion of Larsa was merely an organic continuation of the Elam campaign.

Rim-Sin himself didn't leave his capital, opting to have his brother defend the northern ends of his kingdom. Interestingly, this brother of his also had the name Sin-Muballit, like Hammurabi's father, and his station was at Mashkan-shapir, the same city Rim-Sin's father ruled from. The city, it should be noted, was meant to be the capital of the kingdom both Warad-Sin and Rim-Sin continued to rule. Him opting to stay in Larsa proved to be a bad decision; Hammurabi's coalition troops took hold of Mashkan-shapir, but didn't stop there. Very soon, the region of Yamutbal, also under Rim-Sin's control, felt the sting of the coalition, and not long after that both Nippur and Isin fell under Babylonian dominion. Each of these wins was detrimental to Rim-Sin. Losing Isin to a different ruler took away from Larsa's historic defeat of their rival, but losing Nippur, an important religious site, was a proper political blow which spoke volumes of how weak Larsa actually was before this new threat. The coalition reached Larsa's walls, and for the next six months, they laid siege to it.

Rim-Sin wasn't about to fight Hammurabi alone, and he tried to enlist the help of his ally, a king of a small city-state named Qatna. Even without this monarch's help, Rim-Sin amassed an army that counted in the tens of thousands. Hammurabi, on the other hand, had lots of allies. Mari's troops were still under his command, and the city he had conquered decades prior, Malgium, provided its own soldiers. Yamutbal's troops, which surrendered to Hammurabi a little after his siege of Mashkan-shapir, also went after Rim-Sin, and Hammurabi went a step further in asking Elam for help, the same Elam he had beaten to the dirt the year before (whose king was still alive!). Ishme-Dagan was also contacted for military help. In other words, most of the cities in Upper Mesopotamia wanted Larsa to lose, and Rim-Sin's defeat was inevitable.

Different reports tell different stories of Larsa's last stand. The most accepted version is that the city ran out of food at some point and that Rim-Sin eloped, but was captured and brought before Hammurabi. An additional problem was the Sutean tribes which seized the opportunity to plunder the city during the siege. Hammurabi's troops, under one of Zimri-Lim's generals, took care of them and got appropriate awards for their deeds in the form of land or grain, or both. Hammurabi's treatment of Larsa was surprisingly far more humane than what other rulers might have done during his time. He did tear down the city's walls but decided against plundering the city itself, opting to maintain peace after his conquest. His subsequent acts in Larsa, from 1762 BCE onwards, were all done with the goal of peace in mind; he declared himself a legitimate successor of Rim-Sin rather than outright declaring Larsa his conquered territory, used his throne room to rule over the city, and even built temples in it. Subsequent temples were also built in Zabalam and Ur as a show of goodwill.

However, the citizens of Larsa might not have appreciated Hammurabi as much as he wanted them to. In fact, years after his death would see the rebellion of this city, but never a return to its glory days. Elamites wanted to use this situation to their benefit, even writing letters to Silli-Sin that they would invade Larsa should Hammurabi turn on Eshnunna. And while Elamite invasion of Larsa didn't happen, Hammurabi's turn on Eshnunna very much did.

Victory over Larsa was more than just an outstanding feat for Hammurabi, who had now firmly established himself as a conqueror and a cunning warrior. It was also a turning point in Mesopotamian history, signaling an end to the concept of the city-state. Before his conquests, most of the region was split into powerful cities, either fully or semi-independent, and each of them held sway over others at some point. Hammurabi introduced a new concept to this area, one of a unified empire with a single ruler and a somewhat improved model of the early examples of empires (Eannatum's kingdom, Sargon's empire, Ur III's territory, Shamshi-Adad's kingdom, etc.) which, as large and powerful as they were, didn't have the same sense of unity that remained during and after Hammurabi's reign. The disunion of city-states that was in full swing before the king of Babylon was ending with him.

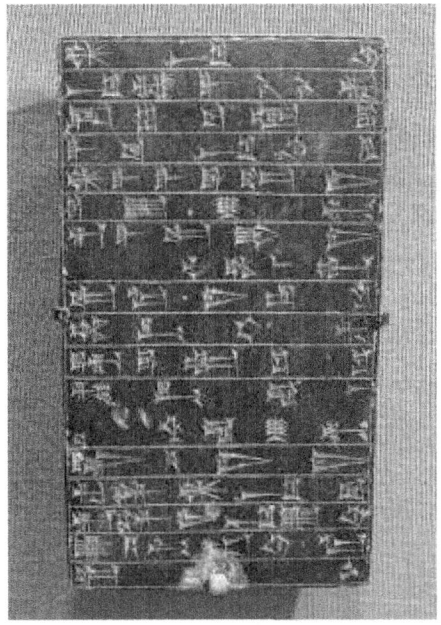

The foundation tablet of Rim-Sin of Larsa, between 1822 and 1763 BCE[ii]

The Defeat of Eshnunna

Eshnunna was probably always going to be one of Hammurabi's targets at some point during his reign. Not only was its geographical position one of great strategic importance, but the region had similar cultural elements to Babylon itself, with the key difference being the city's titular deity, a lesser god known as Tishpak.

During the reign of Sin-Muballit, as well as the early years of Hammurabi, Eshnunna went from a powerhouse to a conquered patch of land in rapid succession. At one point, the ruler of this city was superordinate to even Shamshi-Adad.

Speaking of Shamshi-Adad, it was his death that made the countries of Upper Mesopotamia wage wars for supremacy. This is where the previously mentioned king of Eshnunna, Ibal-pi-el II, becomes a prominent figure. As early as 1776 BCE, he was pressuring Zimri-Lim, a relatively new ruler at the time, to become his ally, or more accurately his subordinate. Zimri-Lim only maintained superficial ties to Eshnunna, opting to maintain Mari's independence instead.

The back-and-forth between Ibal-pi-el and Zimri-Lim eventually led to conflict. Around 1771 BCE, the ruler of Eshnunna sought aid from the tribe of Benjaminites, who were revolting against Mari. Ibal-pi-el sent his troops directly to Mari to assist the rebel tribesmen, and Zimri-Lim had no other choice but to seek aid. Hammurabi responded by sending a regiment, though he didn't do any fighting himself. A treaty ensued between Eshnunna and Mari, with the former remaining in a superordinate position, but not to any noteworthy degree. Zimri-Lim's obligation to Eshnunna amounted to sending statues, servants, and standards as a sign of peace, as well as his promise not to help out Eshnunna's enemies; he didn't even lose any territory from this skirmish.

Elam, as mentioned before, was the force that crushed Eshnunna, with the help of both Mari and Babylon. However, Elamite rule wasn't taken too kindly by the local populace, and when Hammurabi plowed his way through Elam's defenses, the locals in Eshnunna began revolting to the point of an open and hostile rebellion. They swore fealty to Hammurabi and were enough of a problem to Siwe-Palar-Khuppak that he had to focus on them rather than pressing on with his own conquest. But it was in the aftermath of the rebellion where Hammurabi made a critical error—instead of instating a ruler of his choice in Eshnunna, he let the people themselves decide. And the people decided to choose Silli-Sin.

While his name might sound silly (pun intended), Silli-Sin was by no means someone who could be described by that term. He was a commoner, or to be more precise one of the generals in the Eshnunna army. The people chose him for his distinction during the war, and this action itself was somewhat of an anomaly in contemporary Mesopotamia. Simply put, not a lot of commoners reached the position of king, and those that did were freakishly rare. But Silli-Sin nevertheless acted like a proper king. He restored Eshnunna's palace and appointed officials to the cities once held by earlier rulers. In fact, even some of Ibal-pi-el's earlier governors became his subordinates when he came to power.

The relations between Silli-Sin and Hammurabi weren't particularly good. However, the Babylonian monarch wanted to conquer Larsa at the time, so he had to somehow work out an alliance with Eshnunna (a territory he also wanted to conquer). The alliance demanded a treaty between the two cities, and Hammurabi kept sending drafts of this treaty which Silli-Sin kept refusing to acknowledge. Hammurabi continued trying to make Elam his ally throughout this period (a period very shortly after Elam's defeat by his own army), but it ultimately amounted to nothing.

One major breakthrough that finally united Eshnunna and Babylon, at least briefly, was the marriage of Silli-Sin to Hammurabi's daughter. But even this wasn't enough to ensure Hammurabi a smooth conquest of the northern cities. His old ally, Zimri-Lim, wanted more influence politically, but more importantly, he wanted his troops back from Babylon, the same troops that Hammurabi used to crush Elam and Larsa. With that in mind, Zimri-Lim wanted to ally himself with Eshnunna, going so far as to declare them the dominant power. Numerous gifts were exchanged between the two cities, and it was these actions that enraged Hammurabi enough to wage war against both cities.

Considering he no longer had the help of the Mari troops, Hammurabi enlisted new soldiers from Larsa. War preparations were brewing on both sides, with records showing that Silli-Sin wanted control of Shitullum, an important city on the Tigris River. His other noteworthy actions involved bribing Elamite rulers into ignoring the war, allowing for Gutians, his allies, to raid newly-Babylonian Larsa, and asking the northern rulers, all subjects of Hammurabi, not to fulfill their obligations toward him. This, of course, included Zimri-Lim.

Sadly, we don't know too many details of the battle itself, other than the fact that Hammurabi ordered that roughly 2,700 spades and axes be sent to Eshnunna from Larsa. Even the purpose of these tools is unknown in terms of the war itself. However, the result was obvious—in 1762 BCE, Hammurabi crushed Silli-Sin, defeating the Gutians and taking control of Eshnunna.

However, it's important to note what kind of control Hammurabi actually exerted in Eshnunna. Sources suggest that he merely acted as an outside force, giving the city its independence in name only. He didn't incorporate the city into his kingdom and even had to quell a rebellion in 1756 BCE by means of flooding. The best example of his influence over Eshnunna was the fact that he incorporated the city of Mankisum into his kingdom, an important strategic point on the Tigris River that led into Eshnunna and was once under its direct control. And while Eshnunna did suffer some decline, with people moving out and settling into nearby villages, it didn't dwindle fully and was relatively stable throughout Hammurabi's reign and beyond. The fate of Silli-Sin is also unknown. While it's true that he was ousted and probably died soon after, it's unknown whether this happened during the war or at some point after it. Not a lot of details remain in Eshnunna itself, and the other nearby documents, such as those in Mari, don't have any records of this time period.

Nevertheless, this was an important win for Hammurabi. Despite not integrating Eshnunna into his realm, he gained free access to northern regions, allowing him to continue conquering to his delight. The next in line was Mari, but before that Hammurabi had other business in the north.

Terracotta relief of the goddess Ishtar, Eshnunna, early 2nd Millennium BCE[iii]

Northern Kingdoms and Hammurabi

In terms of pure geography and overall historical and cultural backgrounds, what we call Northern Mesopotamia was vastly different from its southern counterpart. After all, the south of this region was home to some of the oldest, most esteemed cities such as Nippur, Ur, Uruk, Lagash, Kish, Larsa, Isin, Sippar, and many others. It was the birthplace of cuneiform writing and culture, as well as religion. In contrast, Northern Mesopotamia had cities that were nowhere near as old or as revered as these. Nevertheless, it maintained a bustling, busy life with its own urban centers, culture, and customs. One colloquial name used at the time for this region was Subartu, a name Hammurabi himself notes as one of the territories he pacified by conquest.

People in the north lived relatively similar to those in the south. They either farmed, fished, or herded cattle for their source of food; they built cities with high walls and temples with esteemed local deities; and they had king lists complete with year names and achievements. More importantly, they were just as involved in the political games of the region as their southern kinsmen.

During Hammurabi's time, this area was under the rule of Shamshi-Adad. As noted, he was such an important ruler that his death left a power vacuum that needed to be filled, and everyone in the north with aspirations of power sought to do this. But Shamshi-Adad didn't die without successors. His oldest son, Ishme-Dagan, was crowned king of his father's capital, Ekallatum. The younger son, Yasmah-Adad, was ruling over Mari before Zimri-Lim's "Reconquista" of this city. By the time Hammurabi began his first war efforts, Ishme-Dagan had become little more than a local prince, governing over Ekallatum and next to nothing else past its walls. Nevertheless, as a descendant of a great ruler, he still maintained a watchful eye on the events that happened around him. He was one of those northern rulers that saw the potential of Hammurabi and decided to put themselves under his patronage. Naturally, Ishme-Dagan didn't always agree with Hammurabi's decisions, but he nonetheless helped out whenever the need arose in Babylon. For example, he sent troops out to help Hammurabi in his fight against Elam in 1764 BCE and maintained relations throughout the war with Larsa. This help of his was probably due to the fact that Hammurabi "forgave" him for an unsubstantiated accusation of stealing goods and riches from Marduk's temple to bring to Elam. Another result of Hammurabi "forgiving" Ishme-Dagan for his alleged transgressions was the fact that his generals were allowed to participate in Hammurabi's secret council meetings, a courtesy the Babylonian monarch didn't even extend to Zimri-Lim of Mari, a far stronger supporter whose army he still held within his city's walls. Zimri-Lim's representatives notified their ruler of this, and the relations between the two kings began to deteriorate with little to no chance of recovery.

During Ishme-Dagan's absence while he was in Babylon helping out Hammurabi with his war efforts, the Elamite general Atamrum (also a supporter of Hammurabi at one point) conspired with local noblemen and plotted to instate Ishme-Dagan's son Mut-Ashkur as the new ruler of Ekallatum. Mut-Ashkur was not of age to rule, and after Elam's demonstrable defeat, Ishme-Dagan returned to his hometown and reclaimed the crown. Strangely, his son wasn't eliminated for participating in this coup, as he still succeeded Ishme-Dagan on the throne later on.

Hammurabi was an ally of Ishme-Dagan, but this relationship they shared slowly began to crumble. Ishme-Dagan did not like how Hammurabi treated the king of Mari better than him, which his messengers made clear to the Babylonian king. In response, he made it clear to them that it was his decision who was to be treated in what way, and that Ishme-Dagan was under obligation to treat Zimri-Lim as a superior. But there was also the question of Atamrum. Prior to this exchange with the messengers of Ekallatum, Hammurabi had sent Atamrum troops numbering close to 300 men. A small number, but a noteworthy one nonetheless. Ishme-Dagan's messengers also made this clear to Hammurabi, but he maintained that the number was insignificant and that Ishme-Dagan was still a friend and ally, which he likely didn't believe himself nor cared about.

Speaking from a position of pure pragmatism, Hammurabi could not afford to send any troops to Ekallatum. After all, it was 1763 BCE, and he was already knee-deep in fighting Larsa. Wasting troops on a nothing-ruler like Ishme-Dagan was beneath him. However, the bigger reason why he didn't do this was the relationship he had with Mari. Zimri-Lim was a ruler on par with Hammurabi in terms of manpower, wealth, and experience. Providing troops that would go after Mari would have been political suicide at that turbulent time, so he kept his distance. Whether he considered Zimri-Lim a proper ally or friend is debatable at best.

Ishme-Dagan, nevertheless, continued to look for ways to fight against Mari and remove himself from Hammurabi's influence. He sought help from Eshnunna, which responded positively but ultimately did nothing of substance to help. The ruler of Ekallatum had far worse problems than Mari or Babylon, however, and they included the distant Zagros-based kingdom of Turukkum and its ruler Zaziya. Namely, Zaziya kept on pestering Shamshi-Adad's successor until, at one point, he proposed a treaty. Naturally, the treaty was a trap, and before he knew it, Ishme-Dagan had to face the sacking of his native Ekallatum, loss of countless goods, livestock, grain—basically anything the invaders could carry with them. Beaten, and without proper support, he once again went to Babylon and sought help from Hammurabi.

But it was evident Hammurabi had had enough. During his campaign against Eshnunna, which ended in a decisive victory, he also sent a contingent of troops (that numbered in the tens of thousands) to sack and "pacify" a whole slew of minor cities in the north. Hammurabi would boast that he held sway over Ekallatum, Zalmaqum, Burunda, Kakmum, and Turukkum. Some of these cities should sound familiar. Besides Ekallatum (which Ishme-Dagan and his descendants continued to rule even after this intervention by the Babylonian monarch), Zalmaqum was another city that had provided help against Elam several years ago. Turukkum, of course, is the city which Zaziya ruled, and even prior to becoming the vassal of the Babylonian king, he praised Hammurabi's skill during the skirmish with the Elamites. Hammurabi persisted in pacifying the region by means of conquest, and in the same year that he sacked Mari, he took direct control of Qattara, one of the few cities that actually fell under Ekallatum's rule at the time. He deposed its king Ashkur-Adad and placed his brother-in-law on the throne instead. This man was named Aqba-Hammu, and just judging on his name alone, you can tell that he was a willing subordinate to Hammurabi. He had even expressed as much by way of his title, which was "servant of Hammurabi," and even referred to himself as such when corresponding with his wife, Iltani. This loyalty extended down to his son Re'um-El as well.

Based on his actions in this period, it's safe to say that Hammurabi sought power, among other things, and while he might not have directly included the sacked cities into his kingdom, he certainly could directly influence their decisions to his benefit. Much like Eshnunna, other cities of the north now had puppet rulers who were at Hammurabi's beck and call, and the few that dared to revolt did so at the expense of their lives.

Ishme-Dagan's name stamped onto a brick found at Ur, currently in London

Mari's Submission

It was, after all, inevitable. After several intense years of intrigue, bloodshed, partnerships broken, and enemies befriended, it was only a matter of time before Zimri-Lim and Hammurabi would cross swords (though not literally, as the two rulers never met face to face).

But before moving onto Mari's fall, it's important to know how Mari rose to where it was. A seven centuries' old city by the time of Zimri-Lim, Mari was an important port located in the middle of the Euphrates valley. Due to this position, it was influenced culturally by several different traditions, most notably those of Babylon and Assyria. In fact, Mari was such a beautiful, awe-inspiring location that Shamshi-Adad chose it as one of his three capitals. This was where he instated his second son, Yasmah-Adad, before dying and leaving the city to its own fate. And its own fate would have the locals rebel, remove Yasmah-Adad from power, and place Zimri-Lim at the top.

Zimri-Lim claimed to be the son of Yahdun-Lim, hence the similarities in their names. Yahdun-Lim's dynasty had ruled Mari before so this familial connection would have given Zimri-Lim a credible claim over the city. However, his father was likely Hadni-Adad, a Banu-Simaal tribesman with no real relation to the native Mariotes. This makes Zimri-Lim similar to Silli-Sin, insofar as neither of the two really came from royalty, yet they took the throne of a major city and distinguished themselves as rulers. Zimri-Lim, in particular, succeeded here, as one can easily put him shoulder to shoulder next to other powerful rulers of the period, such as Eshnunna's Ibal-pi-el II, Larsa's Rim-Sin I, and even Babylon's own Hammurabi.

When it came to Hammurabi, the two rulers maintained a lively correspondence and, at least in the beginning, showed signs of goodwill toward each other. All three of Hammurabi's known sons, the older successor Samsu-iluna and the younger sons Sumuditana and Mutu-Numaha, visited Mari regularly, and entire houses and areas had to be emptied out to accommodate them.

But there was one sore spot which would prove to be the reason behind the later clashes of Babylon and Mari, and that was the city of Hit. Hit was a bitumen-rich place on the Euphrates River, and it was right between the borders of the territories the two cities controlled. Hammurabi used bitumen for his boats, and controlling

Hit would allow him easier access to this material. Mari, on the other hand, held Hit in high regard due to the river's verdict ritual. Namely, if someone was accused of a particular crime, they (or someone representing them) had to perform a task in the Euphrates to prove their innocence. Normally this would include swimming a distance while holding a heavy stone, or swimming a certain distance under the surface of the river. Whatever the task was, the outcome was simple—if you were to bob your head out before completing the task successfully, or if you drowned on the spot, you'd lose and be proven guilty.

In short, one city wanted Hit for spiritual and judicial reasons, the other for practical ones. While Elam was still in power, they presided over cases such as these, and the Elamite king decided in favor of Mari, which Babylon didn't like. However, he couldn't just up and invade Hit, as he had far more pressing matters to tend to, such as defeating Elam and removing its yoke upon the Mesopotamians. For this, he needed Mari as an ally (as well as Larsa and a few other cities, which we covered earlier), and this meant either solving the Hit issue post-haste or shelving it for later. His pressure of Zimri-Lim to relinquish claims over Hit never bore any fruit, as the Mariote leader vehemently refused to do so. A quick treaty was proposed by Zimri-Lim, urging Hammurabi to withdraw his claims until they had dealt with Elam, against which they were now waging full-on war. Hammurabi managed to postpone the Hit issue rather than addressing it, and Zimri-Lim, after consulting diviners, decided not to release his claim of the city either.

During the wars against Larsa, which followed shortly after the defeat of Elam, Zimri-Lim demanded his troops be returned to him, which Hammurabi kept delaying. The two mistrusted each other more than ever, and this was reflected in their foreign policy. Hammurabi received word that his ally Atamrum was assisting Mari behind his back, as well as similar news regarding the cities of Yamhad and Zalmaqum, both allies of Mari and Babylon at some point. The entire thing escalated when each monarch tried to ally himself to Silli-Sin of Eshnunna. Silli-Sin was in a predicament, considering he was the husband of Hammurabi's daughter but that Zimri-Lim willingly accepted his superiority if he were to strike Babylon with him. Hammurabi saw this as the perfect reason behind declaring war on both Eshnunna and Mari, deeming them traitors. Eshnunna was dealt with in 1762 BCE, and nothing was stopping Hammurabi from marching toward Mari and snatching it. Zimri-Lim kept a close eye on Babylon's operations, having planted spies in the court, and just to make sure of his potential victory over Hammurabi, he consulted oracles and got a favorable response. A favorable response that was, as it turned out, horribly wrong.

Hammurabi attacked Mari from the south and the north, prompting Zimri-Lim to take defensive measures. A border-city of Hanat was sacked soon after, by two generals who hated Mari to the bone, no less—those were Mutu-Haqdum and Rim-Adad. Naturally, Hammurabi had a massive army, though most of it probably contained people living in the near vicinity who didn't abide by Zimri-Lim's rules.

No records survive of the final battle between the two cities, but the results are well-known—Hammurabi conquered Mari in 1761 BCE and beat Zimri-Lim, of whose last years on this Earth we know next to nothing. Mari was sacked, with precious treasures, statues, and other objects taken away to Babylon, and its private archives purged. This particular move, probably done for political reasons by Hammurabi's henchmen, proved most disastrous for modern archeology and history, as we're missing the crucial last five months of Mari's correspondence with both Babylon and Mari's allies like Eshnunna and Yamhad. The last time Mari would be mentioned during Hammurabi's reign was two years after the king's conquest of the city. Namely, in 1759 BCE, the Babylonian king had to squash a revolt of the Mariotes, and he did so in the most brutal way which included burning the palace and other buildings to the ground. Other than that, Hammurabi's treatment of Mari remains unknown to us.

Remains of Zimri-Lim's palace in Mari, today's Syria[iv]

Chapter 3 – Reign of Hammurabi: Babylon During His Reign, Relations to Other Cities

Hammurabi's Babylon

As stated, Babylon was little more than a minor city in the north of Mesopotamia before and even during much of Hammurabi's reign. It wasn't even particularly old, at least when compared to others. Four centuries is by no means a small amount of time, but there were even older northern cities than that. Mari, for example, had at that point existed for 700 years.

The fact that we know very little of Babylon's ancient history might additionally highlight how unimportant it was to the contemporary people of Mesopotamia. Even during the first five rulers of the First Babylonian dynasty, the city was merely a successful port. As such, it wasn't strange that outside forces frequently coveted it. Not much could distinguish Babylon from other cities in terms of culture, religion, and literature, considering they worshiped more or less the same pantheon as everyone else, wrote in cuneiform, and had the same institutions to nurture these aspects of their culture. However, ethnically speaking, Babylonians were really descendants of Amorites, and Amorites, like Akkadians and other minor peoples surrounding them, were Semitic, but not the same branch as the Semites already there. In fact, Hammurabi probably never saw himself as "Babylonian" in an ethnical sense, merely as an Amorite.

Him being an Amorite wasn't the only distinguishing feature of Hammurabi as a ruler. His conquests, all done within the span of half a decade, put him front and center. Naturally, he didn't stop with his conquest of Mari, as he had moved on to several minor territories in the meantime. Roughly by his 38th year, he had stopped warring and focused on his territories in a more legal, judicial sense; scholars and researchers typically take this year as the one when he commissioned his now-famous Code of Laws, though this can't be claimed with enough certainty. For a short time, his kingdom was vast, and it was about to be unified by a single set of civil laws.

But Hammurabi did more than conquest in his golden years. In fact, he had spent a good amount of time even prior to the defeat of Elam building and rebuilding temples in various cities. He did the same with canals, including his "magnum opus" in this respect, the canal called "Hammurabi is abundance" which stretched for roughly 160 kilometers or 99.4 miles and spanned several major cities—Ur, Uruk, Larsa, Isin, Nippur, and Eridu.

Not only did this canal (and others that followed) boost his own case with the local populace, but it also made everyone wealthier. More irrigation meant more crops, which meant more food. Also, there was now an easier way to transport goods and people across Hammurabi's vast network of vassal cities and new territories. Just like others before him, Hammurabi made sure to quell the worries of his people by providing them with food and faster mobility.

Babylon was now a center of a major empire. Other powerful centers of power, such as Larsa, were under governors Hammurabi himself appointed. For example, Larsa itself (which Hammurabi all but renamed Yamutbal, the term used for that entire general region) had a Babylonian man called Sin-Iddinam reign over it, and his roles were numerous, largely of a legal nature regarding territorial and land disputes. Even he had subordinate officials that did his bidding, indicating a decent governing structure under Hammurabi's effectively centralized rule.

The reason his rule is only "effectively" centralized instead of outright centralized is simple. While Hammurabi is effectively the progenitor of a totalitarian, autocratic state, the cities he held under control still didn't feel like anything other than their own entities. People living, for example, in Ur or Uruk never saw themselves as Babylonian during his reign, but exclusively as citizens of their native burg. The reasons for this are rather simple, and they largely revolve around the fact that the politics of city-states was several millennia old at this point, and that it was still too early, historically speaking, to have anything closely resembling what we today call a nation state or a country. Religion also played a strong factor in this, as each city had their own titular deity they prayed to. Hammurabi took note of this, of course, and had richly rebuilt and furnished several such temples during his long reign, including temples as far south as Ur.

Of course, Hammurabi had other plans outside of strengthening the religious centers of other cities and instating his vassals as rulers. He was also concerned with having a decent standing army, and conscriptions were in full swing during his busiest five years of non-stop combat. He would punish deserters heavily and reward loyal soldiers handsomely. There were even sets of laws that dealt with soldiers leaving their land to substitutes to tend to it.

Speaking of laws, Hammurabi's principal concern was to bring justice to his new lands, and this had to include some kind of unified code of regulations, or at least a rough estimate of what his subjects could expect from his own brand of justice. However, this will be covered in more detail in the chapter dedicated to Hammurabi's Code.

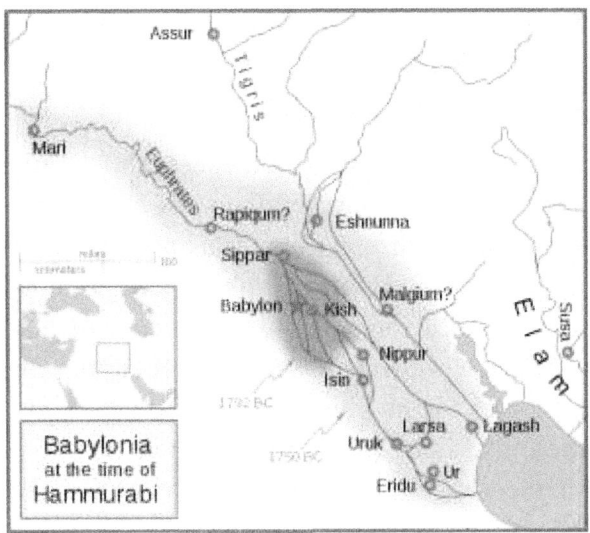

Map of Babylon and nearby cities under Hammurabi's rule[v]

Babylon and Other Cities

Based on what historians have learned from various sources—year names, cylinder seals, correspondences, and even personal names—it's safe to say that Hammurabi's position regarding other cities was, at best, pragmatic and, depending on the situation, at worst duplicitous. The truth probably lay somewhere in the middle, and a definitive answer to this cannot be discerned from the sources we currently have.

If we take the most powerful city-states at the time of not only his reign but his early life as well—those being the kingdom of Shamshi-Adad that included Ekallatum, Mari under either Yasmah-Adad or Zimri-Lim, Elam under Siwe-Palar-Khuppak, Eshnunna of Ibal-pi-el II, and Larsa under Rim-Sin I—we can assume that none of them held any deeply rooted loyalty or kinship to the other. An ally of Mari today could turn on it tomorrow and flock to Babylon, only to go back to Mari the next year and attack Babylon, which would, paradoxically, ally itself to Mari as well. Alliances lasted less than a year, at times even less than a month, and backstabbing was practically the norm. Interestingly enough, this is also the case with minor rulers, such as those of Northern Mesopotamian cities that were either conquered by Hammurabi in his early years or swore loyalty to him after his sack of Eshnunna and Mari.

However, Hammurabi was also known as someone who would regularly rebuild cities, after he had conquered them, of course. He held temples of various states in high regard, and his rebuilding of temples in Ur is an example of this. While it's absolutely possible that this move was purely political on his end and meant to buy favors from the locals, it's also well-known that Hammurabi was very religious, and was serious about illustrating that everywhere. He favored Marduk as the titular deity of his hometown of Babylon, but he also held Shamash, the sun god, in great esteem, as well as the goddess Ishtar.

Naturally, he built (and rebuilt) more than just temples. He would also relieve citizens of their debt and establish new taxes, allowing for some leeway to the people who owed a lot to the local temples and nobles. Next, he made sure everyone grew in wealth by investing in irrigation and repairing existing canals. One perfect example of his treatment of conquered territories is what he did to Larsa. Aside from its walls, he did not sack the city, nor did he exact bloody vengeance upon the citizens. Instead, he ruled from that city during his campaign and invested lots of man-hours and wealth in repairing it. The very next year after the sack of Larsa was dubbed peaceful, despite the military campaigns that followed shortly after.

In short, Hammurabi treated his own territories with care and employed meticulous hard work to elevate them, whereas he saw his neighbors as pawns to be used for expansion. How he thought of his allies will be further explored in the following chapter, but it's safe to say that, at least in some respects, he didn't differ much from his contemporaries.

Chapter 4 – Hammurabi's Character: Physical Appearance, Relations with Other Rulers, Glimpses of His Personality

What Did Hammurabi Look Like?

The short answer is we don't know.

However, we're not here for short answers. Visual representations of Hammurabi exist, though there's only two of them, and they don't really help with this issue. The first of these comes from the bas-relief on top of the very Code of Law that bears his name and, well, the laws themselves. Here we see Hammurabi standing before the sun god, who is seated and providing him with the royal insignia. The same praying pose of Hammurabi is found on the other famous source, a limestone votive inscription probably from Sippar and contemporary to his reign.

Both of these depictions show a very bland, very typical figure of a ruler praying to a deity from whom he's receiving the regalia. The facial features are nothing remarkable, with little proper distinction other than the massive beard, which was common in depicting rulers at the time. In fact, the design of Hammurabi on both of these monuments is grudgingly similar to other reliefs found on monuments dedicated to, or commissioned by, other rulers. In other words, the representations of Hammurabi here are "stock photos" of regular kings during the time of the First Babylonian dynasty.

For a long time, a particular bust of a man, now displayed at the Louvre, held the title "Head of Hammurabi." Sadly, this rather detailed sculpture predates this ruler by several centuries, meaning there was no earthly way that it could represent him.

One clue as to what he might have looked like comes from his Amorite origins. Amorites are described in various sources, including the Hebrew Bible, as looking very European, with fair skin, blue eyes, and reddish hair, and they were apparently very tall. Egyptians would represent them as having slender faces and eagle noses, but the white skin and tall body build remained a constant. If we were to take Hammurabi as a typical Amorite, that's probably what he would have looked like. But again, until we find a definite depiction of Hammurabi from a reliable, contemporary source, we can never be sure.

Votive monument to Hammurabi, between 1790 and 1750 BCE[vi]

Hammurabi's Personality – Dealing with Others

Irritatingly, it's not just Hammurabi's face that we cannot pinpoint; it's also his attitudes, his personal philosophy, his character, and patterns of behavior—in a word, we don't really *know* him.

The easiest action to undertake is to read the sources from his contemporaries, for example, the letters that were sent by either his emissaries or emissaries of his allies or even opponents. The problem with this is the very nature of those letters. It was probably never the case that the king's true words and intentions wound up in a diplomatic letter. He would probably dictate the crux of the message, and his scribes would shift it to fit the purpose of the letter, probably even omitting crucial, if not damning details. Of course, Hammurabi was by no means the sole example of this practice—in the same way, we can't know the real character of Shamshi-Adad, Rim-Sin, Ibal-pi-el, Zimri-Lim, Silli-Sin, Ishme-Dagan, Samsu-iluna, or anyone that Hammurabi came across. Official letters were heavily edited, and would often contain phrases that sounded more "official" and grandiose. In addition, a scribe would never present his ruler in a negative light, nor would he talk about a rival ruler in an entirely positive light either. That makes these letters as evidence to kings' characters rather unreliable and, to put it bluntly, biased.

What we can talk about are the probable, most likely aspects that made Hammurabi what he was. From his reactions to certain situations, such as delays of treaties, lack of military aid, or even dealing with legal issues of the land, we can discern a few slivers of information. Apparently, Hammurabi was heavily involved in the matters of the state, maybe even more so than other rulers. This would make him a diligent, attentive, engaged, and cunning ruler. His cunning can also be discerned in how he dealt with massive diplomatic problems, such as who to support and in what way. He knew how to play his opponents, and wasn't afraid to use those tactics to his advantage. His entire correspondence with either Zimri-Lim or Ishme-Dagan fits as the perfect example of this.

A detail that would appear somewhat often would be that Hammurabi was prone to outbursts of anger, such as when Ishme-Dagan pestered him about his relationship with Zimri-Lim or his reactions to the latter allying himself with his enemies. While these events can be taken as exaggeration and even slander (most of these accounts come from Zimri-Lim's ambassadors and serfs while in Babylon and attending some of the private councils), it's not that far off the mark to assume that Hammurabi would have an emotional moment here or there.

Hammurabi also saw great virtue in religion, and this included the practice of haruspicy, or reading animal entrails to predict the future. He was one of many rulers who would consult auspices and temple priests to try and predict the outcome of a situation by sacrificing a goat and reading its entrails. Again, this practice might come off as typical of any Mesopotamian ruler, especially some that had a direct impact on Hammurabi such as Zimri-Lim, but with Hammurabi, the religiosity of the practice struck harder, or so it seems at least.

In terms of his private life, it's known that he had numerous wives (of whom we don't know a single name) and at least three children. The oldest, Samsu-iluna, would inherit his empire and would probably be the last Babylonian ruler to maintain such a vast territory. All of his sons went to Mari on various occasions, which showed how committed Hammurabi could be when it came to alliances with other states (or, to be precise, how committed Hammurabi appeared).

Chapter 5 – The Code of Hammurabi and Early Mesopotamian Law

Without a doubt, there can be no discussion of Hammurabi without talking about his biggest gift to the world, his famous Code of Laws. This monument has been discussed, dissected, cited, disputed, and discussed anew by experts of so many various fields that it's not an exaggeration to call it one of the most studied pieces of ancient history.

Discovery of the Code

In the winter of 1901 and 1902, a team of French explorers led by Jacques de Morgan was doing excavations at Susa, the ancient capital of Elam. One of the archeologists in their group, an Egyptologist named Gustave Jéquier, found the massive stele containing these laws broken into three easily adjustable pieces. After they reconnected it, the team took it with them, and with some effort, another member of the expedition named Jean-Vincent Scheil translated it and published said translation in 1902. Since then, various other translations appeared, and there are even replicas of the stele in universities around the world.

It should be noted that this stele is by no means the oldest surviving code of laws from ancient times. Three laws that we know of predate it, and they include the Code of Ur-Nammu, the Laws of Eshnunna, and the codex of Lipit-Ishtar, and they were found in Ur, Eshnunna, and Isin respectively. However, the age of the code isn't the only detail about it which has modern misconceptions surrounding it, but we'll discuss that further at the end of this chapter

The Appearance of the Stele

The stele containing the Code is made of black diorite and stands a little over 2.2 meters, or 7.5 feet tall. At its top stands a bas-relief of Hammurabi in a praying position, while seated before him is the sun god Shamash, providing him with the royal insignia and thus letting us know that the ruler was chosen by the gods to impose justice upon the land. Some speculate that the god might actually be Marduk, but the iconography of the seated deity aligns more with Shamash, hence why it's widely accepted that he's providing Hammurabi with his regalia. On top of that, even in Sumerian days, Shamash or Utu was the god of justice; therefore, it makes more sense that he would be on the stele. To top it all off, Hammurabi actually worshiped Shamash as much as he did Marduk and even rebuilt his temples across his vast kingdom.

This bas-relief of the two figures only takes up roughly a fourth of the stele. The rest is filled to the brim with columns of cuneiform writing, detailing probably close to 300 laws. We say "probably" because a notable portion of them is missing, erased by a later ruler in an attempt to add their own (a practice Hammurabi was aware of while he was commissioning the steles). Despite this huge gap, it can safely be said that this monument is one of the longest ancient texts to be translated, and is also one of the most intact. If we compare, for instance, the *Epic of Gilgamesh*, it took multiple different sources from several ancient cities, sometimes hundreds of miles away, to make sense of the missing parts of the epic, and it is still missing a huge chunk.

The Code of Hammurabi; the top shows the Babylonian king standing before the sun-god Shamash[vii]

The Composition of the Code

Possibly the most interesting part of the Code is how it was comprised. It doesn't necessarily read as just a code of law if you take its prologue and epilogue into consideration.

Speaking of, the Code is usually divided into three distinct sections. The two mentioned in the paragraph above are the prologue and the epilogue, both written as poems and both having an exalted air to them. The mid-section contains the laws, and they deal with various, largely civic topics. Historians usually divide them up further by their stated topic or purpose, and those are as follows: legal and judicial proceedings, property offenses, real estate issues, financial deals and arrangements, inheritance and marriage (in particular involving women), assault, professional fees and responsibilities of those receiving them, agricultural issues, hiring rates, and slavery. Naturally, a huge portion of laws, some 40 or so in total, is missing between those dealing with real estate and those dealing with financial arrangements, so we can't exactly say what they contained, though judging by the proximity of the topics they would fit between, it's highly likely that they dealt with those two as well.

Social Stratification of Babylonians

Before moving onto the Code proper, we should address an important detail regarding social classes in Hammurabi's Babylon. The typical three classes of people listed in various sources are awilum, mushkenum, and wardum. Each of these is somewhat problematic to explain without understanding the context of Babylonian life, and even then, it's somewhat hard to discern. Wardum were slaves, but not in the typical sense. A slave could, theoretically, buy or earn back his freedom, and the term could even refer to a man indebted to a different man for a short time span. Mushkenum is possibly the most difficult of the three to explain, as it represents free men who worked at the palace, but who could get the king's property in usufruct without keeping it (in other words, they could work on it, reap its goods, but couldn't destroy or damage it). Awilum would be landowners who did not have to rent anything nor rely on any higher authority for what they owned. These last two classes are problematic in the sense that there wasn't a clear distinction between them or at least none that was explained in the sources we have available to us. This is frustrating because the laws listed in the Code heavily depend on what level of social hierarchy the accused or the accuser was a part of.

Chapter 6: Dissecting the Code

As stated, multiple translations were used throughout the last century when it came to Hammurabi's Code. The one we'll be using is the version translated by Leonard William King in 1915. Though newer and more detailed translations exist, this one has been cited in English scientific literature the most.

The Prologue

Hammurabi's Code begins with a lengthy poem which speaks of his achievements, his favor with the gods, and the lands that he rules over. Its opening lines are roughly as predictable as one expects. At first, he invokes the gods of Mesopotamia, including "Anu the Sublime" and his "Anunnaki" (i.e., the children of Anu), Bel ("lord of Heaven and Earth"), Marduk, Ea, and many others, mentioning how they made Babylon great upon their arrival. Of course, those selfsame gods chose Hammurabi himself as the rightful—and righteous—leader of all "black-headed people" between the two rivers. It was, according to the gods, his task to be "like Shamash" and to "enlighten the land" for the continuing well-being of humanity.

Invoking the will of the gods in order to justify the ruler's right to govern the land is a staple of ancient Mesopotamia. With these lines, Hammurabi mentions, in almost a single breath, how the gods chose his city, Babylon, to be the greatest out there, how they chose Marduk to be the most exalted among the Anunnaki or the Igigi (the two might be synonymous), and—of course—how they chose Hammurabi himself to act as the arbiter of justice in said exalted city in the name of the said exalted god. It's important to bear in mind that Anu was the father of all creation in ancient Mesopotamia, so Hammurabi is effectively saying that he was chosen by existence itself to propagate justice to Man.

But Hammurabi remembers to be just humble enough not to appear arrogant. He stresses that his laws are here "so that the strong should not harm the weak" and that his goal, aside from ruling over the black-heads, i.e., Mesopotamians (though earlier, this was referring to Sumerians specifically), is to bring righteousness to the land and to destroy the wicked. His goal, in other words, is a noble one.

The sheer mountain of text that follows details everything he had done up to that point in his life. He had done repairs on many temples and canals. He then enriched and rebuilt cities such as Nippur, Eridu, Babylon, Ur, Sippar, Larsa, Uruk, Isin, Kish, Kutha, Borsippa, Dilbat, Kesh, Lagash, Girsu, Adab, Akkad, Ashur, and Nineveh, and even lists all of the temples within them, including the deities that inhabit them. It's also not surprising that he styles himself "the king of four quarters" and "the king of the land of Sumer and Akkad," as this was the title many rulers had before him, both those that rightfully deserved it and those who merely tacked it on to bolster their ego despite not having the territory to match said title. Hammurabi did, indeed, unite "the four quarters," with the exception of a few independent cities, so his use of the title is technically just.

Not being one to understate his importance in bringing justice, Hammurabi ends his prologue with these words:

When Marduk sent me to rule over men, to give the protection of right to the land, I did right and righteousness in . . . , and brought about the well-being of the oppressed.

Law code of Hammurabi, a smaller version, terracotta from Nippur, 1790 BCE, currently in London[viii]

The Code Proper

The version used for this book contains 282 laws, of which roughly 40 are missing. The best way to look at them has to be one by one, in succession, as they often build atop the law that preceded them.

The first five laws deal with the judicial process in Babylon, and the very first law tells us an important factoid about legality throughout human history:

1. If anyone ensnare another, putting a ban upon him, but he cannot prove it, then he that ensnared him shall be put to death.

Yes, this law right here deals with the presumption of innocence. Even back in ancient times, lawmakers knew that a person had to be assumed innocent until proven guilty, and it's no wonder that this law is the very first Hammurabi wants us to see.

It's important to pay attention to this particular law, considering how frequently the current political climate seems to shun the notion of "innocent until proven guilty." This postulate has been around since the earliest of days, and it's no wonder that the right to a fair trial stands as one of the universal human rights. Naturally, the punishment for this transgression is rather harsh, but then again, it's no different than most of the laws within this Code, including the very next one:

2. If anyone bring an accusation against a man, and the accused go to the river and leap into the river, if he sink in the river his accuser shall take possession of his house. But if the river prove that the accused is not guilty, and he escape unhurt, then he who had brought the accusation shall be put to death, while he who leaped into the river shall take possession of the house that had belonged to his accuser.

Again, we have the river verdict ritual in action, the same that the Mariotes used within the city of Hit. The compensation of either party is rather large and strict—whatever the case, one of them will die, and the other will claim the property of the dead man.

Considering the time period, capital punishment wasn't out of the norm, and considering that both of these laws deal with the presumption of innocence (in their own way, of course), it just goes to show how seriously Babylonians took this concept.

The next two laws are an example of how one law builds upon the other, and are merely the first in line of dozens that do so throughout the Code:

3. If anyone bring an accusation of any crime before the elders, and does not prove what he has charged, he shall, if it be a capital offense charged, be put to death.

4. If he satisfy the elders to impose a fine of grain or money, he shall receive the fine that the action produces.

Once again, we're dealing with the presumption of innocence, but for the first time, we get a glimpse of a potential legal proceeding, i.e., a certain council of "elders." In ancient Mesopotamia, most legal and military matters had to be decided on by a set of two councils, one made up of elders, another of younger, yet prominent men of the city. And once again, we see capital punishment as the resolution of falsely accusing someone of a crime. However, we also see a resolution if the opposite happens, i.e., the council will provide the accuser what he's owed.

The next and final law dealing with judicial proceedings deals with the judges themselves:

5. If a judge try a case, reach a decision, and present his judgment in writing; if later error shall appear in his decision, and it be through his own fault, then he shall pay twelve times the fine set by him in the case, and he shall be publicly removed from the judge's bench, and never again shall he sit there to render judgement.

Babylon did indeed have judges, and these were usually governors or lieutenants picked by the king himself. They would largely deal with smaller matters that didn't require Hammurabi's attention, but considering how often he would micromanage them, they had to do an impeccable job. Otherwise, they would be severely punished, though, as we see here, not by death, but by way of compensation and a layoff.

These five laws lay the foundation of Babylonian legal thought and are not as specific as the ones that follow. They do serve as a shining example of how committed Hammurabi was to maintaining truthfulness and justice, and especially truthfulness *in* justice.

The following twenty laws deal with property offenses, and each come with their own separate category. For example, laws 6-14 speak of theft, be it of animals, goods, or even people. Stealing from the temple or the court would bring death upon the thief, as well as the man who got stolen goods from him (6); the same fate awaited someone who bought silver, gold, male or female slaves, sheep, oxen, asses, or anything else from anybody without a witness or a contract (7). Stealing cattle from the temple would force a thief to pay thirty times the sum, yet it was only ten times for stealing from a free man (8). Naturally, death awaited him if he couldn't provide the payment. It was a bit more complicated if someone lost an item, for instance, and someone else found it. Law 9 states that the person claiming that a merchant sold it with witnesses at hand must prove so by bringing the said witnesses and the merchant. The owner was also ordered to bring his own set of witnesses, in case they could identify that the stolen property was really his. The judge was to examine who was telling the truth. If the merchant was the thief, he was killed, and the man received his property back, whereas the person who bought stolen goods received some money from the late merchant's estate. The next three laws, namely 10, 11 and 12 (13 is missing) expand on law 9. If a buyer of the stolen item couldn't get any witnesses, he was the one guilty of thievery and got the death sentence. If the presumed owner was the one lying, the same fate awaited him as well. However, each of the aggrieved parties had roughly half a year to get witnesses, and should any of them fail to do so, they were dubbed the culprit and were put to death.

Law 14 is a bit different from these, though it also deals with stealing. It demands that any thief of a "minor son" must be put to death. It isn't as detailed as the laws before it, but it fits well with the theme and has the appropriate punishment to match the others.

Stealing was a crime; however, stealing from the temple was a particularly egregious offense. Temples were considered houses of the gods, and the statues there were considered as gods themselves, manifested on Earth. As such, taking temple property was effectively stealing from the gods themselves, and nothing less than a death penalty would follow. The same punishment went for anyone who received stolen goods as a gift or who bought them.

Of course, these goods included sheep, cattle, oxen, donkeys, grain, statues, slaves of both genders, and just about anything of value. However, we see a discrepancy in terms of class; a thief was to pay less to a free man than he was to the temple or the court, meaning that justice, indeed, favored the wealthy. However, it still didn't favor the perpetrators.

Once more we see the element of bearing false witness, but this time in terms of lost and found property. It also deals with providing witnesses and setting dates for their eventual inclusion into the legal process.

Runaway slaves are the topic of the following six laws. The 15th law states that people taking slaves of either gender from the court or from a free man outside of the city would get the death penalty. The same went for those who received runaway slaves and did not let the proper authorities know that they did; keeping runaway slaves was just as bad as stealing them from others (16).

Of course, some rewards were given to the folks who found runaway slaves and brought them to their masters. Each person would get two shekels of silver as a reward for this act (17; it's important to note that a shekel is an old unit of measurement whose name is currently used as that of Hebrew currency). But there were also times when slaves would refuse to name their old masters, which would prompt an investigation (18). The palace dealt with these, and if the master was found, the slaves would be returned to him. Naturally, keeping these slaves within the house of the person who found them still resulted in death (19), which is a bit redundant of the law, considering that an earlier law had the same contents that issued the same punishment. But there was an area where the finder of the slaves could get away from that punishment. If a slave was to run away from this man, all he had to do was swear an oath to the owners that they ran off, and he was safe (20).

This is an interesting set of laws because it's the first to deal with slaves directly, and it also shows us a little of how Babylonians viewed slaves. Helping and colluding with a runaway slave, much like liberating one without the express permission of their master, resulted in death, yet bringing back a slave could get a lucky Babylonian an award from the master. What appears as a loophole is apparently also part of the law, namely that the slave could run away and that the person whom he ran from merely had to swear to the owners that he did so. It's difficult to imagine that this particular loophole wasn't used to liberate slaves at the time—after all, you only had to swear on your life that the slave overpowered you and fled, and you're scot-free.

The final five laws of this section deal with break-ins and robberies. Law 21 states that if a person was to break a hole into someone's house to steal something, he was killed right then and there at the hole itself. Robbers that committed their crime without having to "put holes in walls" were also put to death according to the law following this one. But with law 23, we see what happens if the thief was somehow not caught. The whole local community would then offer reparations for the stolen goods, and all the person who lost them had to do was swear the amount stolen under oath before the gods. For any slave stolen, law 24 states that the community and someone else unspecified (due to the damage of the code, this particular section of the text is missing) pay one mina of silver to this person's relatives and close family (a mina is another unit often used in ancient Babylon, amounting to 1.25 pounds or 0.57 kilograms). Curiously, law 25 deals with fire, but not with the loss of property to flames; rather, it mentions people stealing things during the process of putting out the fire. A person who stole anything during this horrific event was, rather severely, thrown into that same fire as punishment.

Most of these laws can be linked to what was already said about stealing. As it was established, taking someone's property was punishable by death, and the same went for people doing it while breaking into someone's estate. An interesting detail here deals with not knowing who the perpetrator is. While a section of these laws is missing, it can safely be inferred that the community was to help the victim via compensation, be it for material goods or slaves. That sounds like an interesting way of preventing robberies—if everyone in a district had to pay for what one person did, nobody would dare commit a crime, lest they had to either pay the man back anyway or, if found out, die for their crimes.

It's also odd how specific the law about robberies during house fires is. Considering its specificity, it's safe to assume that these kinds of fires (and these kinds of break-ins) happened often and that something had to be done about it, legally speaking. Naturally, the fitting punishment is about as cruel as any other thus far.

Real estate is the following topic, and within that, a massive 27 laws deal with land tenure alone. According to the first few of these laws, a general or a common soldier did not have gone to war by himself, as he could hire a mercenary. However, failure to compensate the mercenary after the war would result in death and property transfer to the man he hired.

Laws numbered 27, 28, and 29 deal with men captured during the war. If they were to return, the man maintaining their property was to give it back. Alternatively, the man's son or mother could maintain it instead. 30 and 31 deal with the "term limits" of property maintenance—should the original owner return within a year, he would get his original property back from the man he hired, but if he came back after three years, the other man got his property. Then we have 32, which oddly stipulates that a man purchased by a mercenary in battle could not buy his freedom by giving away his property. He was either to pay for it himself or to allow the temple or the court to buy him out. Two more laws past this one deal with mercenaries and prisoners of war, but they are too broken to understand properly.

Laws pertaining to the property given by the king were pretty clear when it came to selling the property to others. Law 35 states that anyone who purchased sheep or cattle that the king had given to his chieftains had to lose his money. The next law deals with the fields, gardens, and houses of anyone, be they nobles, free men, or men working under quit-rent conditions. None of these could be sold under the law. Indeed, law 37 specifically states that any contract tablet made including the contents from the previous law was to be broken, which meant annulment of the whole purchase. Think of it as tearing up a legal document today, or shredding it asunder in a paper shredder. The person who sold these was also to lose his money, with the goods returned to the proper owners.

Oddly enough, nobles and free men couldn't outright sell their property, and if they tried, they got their money back. They would have similar difficulty when it came to assigning tenure of their property to a female relative, such as a wife or a daughter—unless they bought additional property, or if they sold it to an official. Law 38 says just as much, highlighting that the tenure of fields, gardens, or houses could never fall to the wife, the daughter, or to anyone else outside of the house. This attitude, however, changed if the field, garden, or house were something he had bought and held as property. In other words, any new material or "mortgage" possessions were fair game in terms of giving them to female relatives. The same applied when it came to selling said goods to members of the royal family or other noble subjects. Both of these acts—assigning them to the ladies or the nobles—are described in laws 39 and 40.

Indeed, property was no small thing in Hammurabi's Babylon, hence why it was so difficult to either obtain or sell it. It's also not surprising that the royal court handled most of the matters of private property, in particular, the property lent by the king.

The laws continue onward, talking about putting up fences in fields (41) and how to deal with people who either tilled a field poorly (42), failed to do it outright (43), or failed to make an infertile field arable after having offered to do otherwise (44). We can see that most of those laws stated compensation as punishment, both in grain and in forced manual labor. In other words, if you don't plow the field, you'll pay the field owner's fee and be forced to plow it again anyway.

The 45th law interestingly deals with damages caused by forces of nature. A man could rent his field to a tiller at a fixed price and receive this rent, but the bad weather (provided by the gods, of course) could wreck the harvest. The tiller was then held responsible for the damage.

This was somewhat of a dire situation for the tiller because he effectively had to suffer for something outside of his power, such as a storm or any kind of rotten weather destroying the crops. Tillers would, however, benefit if the owner didn't get a fixed rental for his field (46); in that situation, they would split the grain amongst themselves. Owners of fields also had no right to complain if other tillers plowed the field other than the one he hired (47), as he would nevertheless get the grain.

Storms come back in the 48th law, but this time as a beneficial circumstance. Namely, if a person owed something, and the grain he grew to repay the debt was destroyed by bad weather, drought, or even poor soil, his debt was forgiven to him by the creditor, and the "debt-tablet," i.e., the official document dictating the terms of his debt, was to be "washed…in water." That year, the tiller's property would be rent-free.

Forgiving debts and loans was the bread and butter of every Mesopotamian ruler as early as the first Sumerian kings. Having a law specifically addressing debt write-offs is a strategic plus, as it lets the subjects know that there are situations beyond their control which provide a good excuse for not paying debt.

The last four laws of this section deal with obtaining money from a merchant and returning said money in grain the merchant was to plow, but it has an interesting detail to it:

49. If any one take money from a merchant, and give the merchant a field tillable for corn or sesame and order him to plant corn or sesame in the field, and to harvest the crop; if the cultivator plant corn or sesame in the field, at the harvest the corn or sesame that is in the field shall belong to the owner of the field and he shall pay corn as rent, for the money he received from the merchant, and the livelihood of the cultivator shall he give to the merchant.

50. If he give a cultivated corn-field or a cultivated sesame-field, the corn or sesame in the field shall belong to the owner of the field, and he shall return the money to the merchant as rent.

51. If he have no money to repay, then he shall pay in corn or sesame in place of the money as rent for what he received from the merchant, according to the royal tariff.

52. If the cultivator do not plant corn or sesame in the field, the debtor's contract is not weakened.

An average person would think that Mesopotamians couldn't grow corn, considering it is native to the Americas, and they would be right—the "corn" in these laws refers to grain in general. From these laws, we can see that a field owner had various ways of repaying a merchant for the lent money, almost all of them referring to the grain the very field he lent the merchant produced.

Laws numbered 53 through 58 all deal with irrigation negligence and unauthorized grazing, or in other words, irresponsible dealings with property. The first four let us know that flooding a field, be it the accused man's field or that of his neighbors, was an offense that required material compensation: he either had to provide grain or pay a certain amount of grain for each measure of land destroyed by water. Alternatively, he had to sell a vast portion of his property and share the earned money with the man whose field he had flooded.

The remaining two laws deal with shepherds having to pay penalties for their sheep grazing without permission on private property.

59-65 are the last laws before a major break in the text, and they concern orchard cultivation. We learn that cutting down trees in orchards of others is punishable by way of payment (59), that working on the field for five years meant that the owner and the gardener would split the property (60), and that empty patches of land also became property of the gardener eventually (61). We also learn that the gardener had to compensate the owner should he have planted grain on his land and cultivated it (62), that the owner had to pay the gardener should he turn infertile land into an arable one (63), that gardeners got one third of produce for their service (64), and that he had to pay an estimate of produce from other orchards as compensation for the wasted produce in the orchard he was working on (65).

After the notable break, the next law is marked by the number 100, as agreed upon by most historians. This and the following 26 laws all concern financial arrangements within Babylon and are further subdivided into three categories. The first deals with loans, interests, agreements between merchants, and what women innkeepers were allowed to do when loaning goods.

Laws 100 and 101 are clearly linked and deal with interest upon meeting or failing to meet a certain agreement. However, the first part of the 100th law is missing, so we can't be sure what it was about specifically. Laws 102-107 are rather clear, though. Law 102 states that a broker had to repay the debt to the merchant who had entrusted it to him should the broker lose what he borrowed. The very next law mentions an exception to this, and it deals with a thief. The broker who lost his money to robbery had to swear an oath to the gods that this had happened to him, which would render him free of having to pay back the merchant. Moving on to law 104, we learn that for each transaction having to deal with grain, wool, oil, or really anything else, the broker had to take a receipt from the merchant with the exact amount that he had borrowed. After the repayment, he also had to get a receipt to verify the whole deal. This means that both men were bound by law to provide each other with documents about their transactions. A failure from the broker to get a receipt is outlined in law 105, whereas law 106 speaks of what happens if the broker tried to deny the receipt that was agreed upon. The merchant had to swear an oath, and the broker had to pay him three times what he originally agreed on. Law 107 gives us the other side of this argument. In case the merchant was the one cheating the broker, he had to swear an oath as well, but if he still denied his misdeed, he was to pay six times the original sum.

Losing money was a major deal, and anyone who did so had to repay it, especially if said money was entrusted upon them. However, again we see a loophole, one of "swearing unto God that an enemy took it," which allowed for freedom. One way to ensure the fairness of trade was for the agent, who was reselling or redistributing the goods of the merchant, to write down everything and provide the earned amount to the merchant, alongside the receipt with the amount. This would probably be one of the earliest examples of legalizing the use of financial records, an element which would make trade just as important as food production or raw material excavation.

The laws also clearly take into account the potential errors or problems that can arise between the trading parties. An agent had to take the receipt, and the merchant had to acknowledge it. Otherwise, the penalties, while not as cruel as the ones of earlier laws, were devastating for their livelihoods—after all, paying three or six times of any sum is not a laughing matter. Yet again, we see the element of swearing oaths to the gods and invoking divine justice. However, there's the added element of "witnesses and judges." This might not be clear from these laws themselves, but the oaths could have been deemed false by the judges and the public court. What the punishment for this was isn't clear, as it wasn't "codified" on this stele.

The following four laws, intriguingly enough, deal with women as tavern keepers or wine sellers, and they are a mixed bag of good and not-so-good when it comes to dealing with these ladies:

108. If a female tavern-keeper does not accept corn according to gross weight in payment of drink, but takes money, and the price of the drink is less than that of the corn, she shall be convicted and thrown into the water.

109. If conspirators meet in the house of a tavern-keeper, and these conspirators are not captured and delivered to the court, the tavern-keeper shall be put to death.

110. If a "sister of a god" open a tavern, or enter a tavern to drink, then shall this woman be burned to death.

111. If an inn-keeper furnish sixty ka of usakani-drink to . . . she shall receive fifty ka of corn at the harvest.

These laws are, if anything, pretty cut and dry. If she overprices the drinks, she'll end up drowning. If she harbors the enemies of the state, she dies. And if she was to provide a certain amount of drink (60 *Ka*, in this case; Ka or Qa is a unit of liquid measurement which equals roughly 1kg/2lbs of water in a cube whose edges are 10.2cm/4in long) on credit, she was to be compensated for it during a harvest.

But the most interesting of these laws is 110, as it deals with a high priestess opening or drinking within a tavern. It's a common misconception that women were treated almost like slaves during these times in history. While they weren't as revered as men in higher positions of power, they were far from being at the bottom. The best examples are the various classes of priestesses that made up the royal court. They would often serve as wives or sisters of gods, and as such played vital roles in sacred rituals such as marriages and child-rearing. They were also allowed to own land, and even before Babylon's ascendance to power, were even able to reach positions of power as "kings."

All of this is important to keep in mind when discussing law 110 of Hammurabi's Code. A priestess was a position not to be taken lightly, and any woman who held the title wasn't allowed to stoop to such a level as to open a tavern or an inn since it was a more earthly place where people regularly got drunk. And speaking of getting drunk, a high priestess who was intoxicated, or even inebriated, was one that stomped on the sacred beliefs of old Babylonians. Sacrilege was never punished by anything short of death, and even the highest classes weren't immune to this, whichever of the two genders they were. Women enjoying the tavern life, however, must have been a frequent phenomenon during Hammurabi's reign, considering the law pertaining to this activity earned a spot on the stele. More laws dealing with women specifically will come, but not just yet—we still have debt and deposits of grains and other goods to cover.

Debt and one's obligation to it are covered in laws 113 to 119, with law 112 deviating from this group of laws and the one preceding it, as it deals with the safekeeping of money and what happens if one who should return it doesn't. In terms of the laws that follow, a man who was owed grain wasn't allowed to take it by himself, or else he was to return the amount he took and annul the debt (113). He was also not allowed to falsely accuse someone of debt and was to recompense him for every sum he took (114). Things also didn't look good for the man who was owed money or grain if the person who had to return it to him died (115), because the case would automatically be annulled. It then becomes interesting when social class is made part of the debt; an imprisoned man who was under debt, if he were tortured or mistreated and died thereafter, could cost his imprisoner either his life (if he was born a free man) or an amount of money (if he were a slave to begin with). Social differences, therefore, played a major role in how the law was implemented, and the lower the class of the "victim," the less severe the penalties.

Slavery is covered in the last three laws of this subsection. Law 117 deals with the length of time an indentured slave was to serve his master. A man could sell either himself, his spouse, or his children of either gender, and the time they had to work under their master could not go over three years. Naturally, not everything was that "good" for the slaves; law 118 states that the new master could sell these new slaves to a different master for money and that the slaves had no real say in it, nor did their family members. But then comes law 119, which deals with maidservants who bear children to the men of the house. If a man was to sell one to a buyer, the buyer got an immediate refund, while the maidservant became free of her plight.

Three years of forced servitude sounds like a decent deal, considering how slaves were treated in Egypt or ancient Greece, for example. However, slaves also had the misfortune, as we can see, of being resold to others, so technically that could reset their three-year "contract." It's another spectacular loophole, but this time, it worked against the everyday folks, unlike the ones regarding oaths to gods.

The practice of depositing money or grain was just as common in this time as banking is nowadays. The seven laws that follow detail the process completely. Law 120 notes the consequences of what happened to someone who either denied the service of housing grain, stole the grain he agreed on housing, or if there was any damage done to it. The owner had to swear an oath before the gods, and the person housing the corn had to compensate him—in grain, of course. The next law states that the storage rate of every five Ka of grain was to be paid one gur; since gur, as a unit of measurement, is mentioned more prominently in later laws, we will leave out its explanation for now. Law 122 states what a person had to do beforehand when he or she decided to put something up for safekeeping. Naturally, it involved drawing up a contract and having a witness present. The consequences of not having a witness or a contract are evident in law 123—should the person claim safekeeping of the grain (or gold, silver, or really anything of value), without evidence, the courts could just dismiss them in favor of the person doing the uncontracted safekeeping. Then we have law 124, which covers what happens if a safe keeper denied his service, despite the client having a witness to their deal. In this case, the safe keeper had to pay the full price to the aggrieved party. Then there's laws 125 and 126 which cover thieves and safe kept property. In case a thief or a robber stole something from a safe keeper, it was the duty of that same safe keeper to compensate the owner of the property. However, the owner himself had to do his best to find the thief and retrieve what was stolen. The following law states that there are men who might lie that they lost property. If they were to swear an oath before the gods, even if they had no property stolen to begin with, they would be compensated as if they did.

These laws, as we can see, take into account the destruction of the storage space, denial of service, theft (all under law 120), the price for storage (121), the process of acquiring storage space involving witnesses and contracts (122), and the consequences if any of the two were lacking (123); denial of service even with existence of witnesses and the contract also entailed penalties (124), making these four laws essentially one major law separated "thematically." Law 125 deals with theft of property left for safekeeping a bit differently; compensation is a major part of it, but the owner of the house was still under obligation to locate the thief and try to reclaim his property thusly. While this law seems to be rather sober and well-thought up, the very next one, 126, presents another major loophole in Babylonian law. Again, we see the infamous "oath before God" section, and the phrase "even though he has not lost them" rings ominously. We cannot understate that the possibility of this law being misused must have been frequent, if not even commonplace. At any time, anyone who owned property legally could lose it to a random stranger, and all it took was for the stranger to claim before the gods that the property of the owner was actually the property "stolen" from him. Hammurabi's Code was spectacular, but it was clearly far from perfect.

The next section is by far the longest, containing 67 separate laws, all dealing with one common subject—matrimony and everything regarding family. It won't surprise you to hear that a good portion of these laws talk about women and children, which means that this section is possibly the biggest collection of laws regarding the fairer sex in ancient Mesopotamia.

The first two laws, 127 and 128, deal with false accusations and what makes a marriage valid. Law 127 states that if anyone was to "point a finger," i.e., slander someone's wife or a "sister of a god" (temple priestess) without proof, he was to be branded. The law that follows clearly states that the wife who "has no intercourse" with her husband isn't really his wife, legally speaking.

The first law clearly favors women, though of course it specifies priestesses and wives. Branding a slanderer might not be as severe as a death penalty or confiscation of property, but it was a difficult punishment on a whole different level. If branded, a man would effectively become an outcast in his own community.

Now the latter law is interpreted a bit differently, as it also translates to *"if a man take a wife and do not arrange with her the proper contracts, that woman is not a legal wife"*; whichever is correct, it openly tells us how a couple was to marry legally. Once more we can see that women enjoyed a substantial level of justice under Hammurabi and his contemporaries.

The four laws that follow deal with adultery in general, and an eagle-eyed observer can notice a familiar motif in one of them. When reading law 129, we learn that someone's wife who was caught cheating had to be thrown into the water tied up, as was the case with the man she cheated on her husband with. However, the husband had the right to pardon his wife if he wanted to. Law 130 is more inclined to women, as it states that a virgin (either a child or an unmarried soon-to-be bride) who was violated in her home by a man other than her potential husband was innocent of the matter, whereas the man who did that to her was to be sentenced to death. A man could also accuse his wife of adultery, but, as law 131 points out, if she wasn't caught cheating, she was to swear an oath to the gods and go about her day free of any charge. Bizarrely, law 132 states that if a wife was accused of adultery by others, she had to jump into the river for her husband despite her potential innocence.

The first two of these laws are standardly brutal; however, both have a silver lining in terms of pardons (129) or exemption from blame due to the particular circumstances of the case (130). Law 131 again brings up the idea of "swearing/taking an oath," and this time it's the wife who can reap the benefits of a loophole and evade a crime.

The interesting law is 132, just because of how openly it works against the wife, despite her blame. The court of public opinion must have been a powerful tool even back then, considering that this law prescribes her to throw herself to her death to maintain the honor of her husband. This would be one example of a woman properly getting the short end of the legal stick in Babylon, and one of the rare ones where a completely innocent woman could die simply because others pointed their finger at her.

Four more laws follow that specifically deal with the wife, this time talking about her remarriage and when it can come about. Wives of captured husbands had to take care of the estate, and any woman who went to a different man was to be thrown into the water (law 133). However, she had zero blame if the house had no maintenance arranged in advance (134), and if she was to bear children to a different man in this case, she would return to her first husband (upon his own return from war imprisonment, of course) while the children remained with their biological father, i.e., the head of the house the wife went to during her husband's POW days (135). The wife also had full right not to return to her husband if he were to desert his city and thus betray it (136).

The topic of divorce, which covers laws 137 to 143, is a spectacular section, as it uncovers the practice of marriage annulment dating back several thousands of years before our time. And right off the bat, we see that the ladies, under divorce, had it good if they had children with the man who wanted to divorce them. The first law,

law 137, states that if a man wanted separation from a mother of his children, whether she was his wife or concubine, he was to give that woman her dowry as well as a part of the field, garden, and property. That way she could rear children more easily. Once these children grew up, they got a portion of this dowry and these lands. She received an amount equal to that of one son, and after all of that, she could marry whomever she wanted.

That's right—even back then, the wife was properly compensated, even after the adulthood of her children. The following three laws dictate what a man should give his divorcee in case she had borne him no children: it was either an equivalent of her dowry from back when they married (138) or a single *mina* of gold in case no dowry was given (139). However, that amount decreased to a third if the man divorcing said wife was a free man (140).

The following two laws deal with neglect on the part of either partner. If the wife had been neglecting her duties, the husband could either set her free without the dowry or, alternatively, keep her around as a maidservant while bedding a second wife. Law 141 is pretty clear on this: wives weren't just marriage partners. They had their obligations, and not keeping up with them resulted in the penalty outlined above. Consequently, according to 142, a husband who misbehaved toward a hard-working wife must, if proven guilty, pay her the dowry back and let her go live with her original family. Sadly, if the woman had proven to be the one who neglected her duties during this accusation (143), she was to be thrown into the water.

A few of the past laws referenced having a second wife. This is discussed in further detail with laws 144-149. The first of these deals with a wife's maidservant bearing her husband children. If she did, the man wasn't allowed to take on a second wife. 145 then states that, should a husband bring in a second wife after the first one was unable to bear him children, he was not to treat this second wife on an equal level with his first. The first, after all, commanded authority over all others. Next, we have law 146, which deals with a maidservant bearing children and assuming equality with the first wife. The husband wasn't allowed to sell this mother of his children, but he could keep her around and "fit" her among the other maidservants of the house. The following law makes it clear that the husband could sell the maidservant if she bore him no children. Law 148 is just as favorable to the first wife as the ones before it, wherein a woman racked with an illness cannot be sold or removed from the house. The husband had to take care of her until the end of her days. However, the last in this line of laws stipulates that this woman racked with illness doesn't have to stay and that the husband ought to compensate her for the dowry provided by her father, whom she could return to if she wished after the compensation was over.

The first two laws are pretty clear on the authority of the first wife—the husband was not to force her out, nor could he take a different wife if she was to bear him children. In the rare case that the wife couldn't give birth, she would not be merely discarded, as her authority in the house was still above that of a concubine, even if this concubine gave birth to children. If a concubine that bore children assumed an equal status with the wife, the husband had no right to sell her, as he was to keep her around as a maidservant. Compensation once again plays an important role in terms of the original wife leaving the household for one reason or another.

With these laws, we see clearly how different classes were treated differently by the judiciary system. Even if the maidservant was to rise above the wife, she was still treated worse. Time and time again, it was wealth rather than gender differences that subjugated people around the globe and throughout history.

The three laws that follow (150, 151, and 152) all deal with what the wife had to do with the estate after her husband died. She was not to pay any of his debt (though had to pay her own), and the estate didn't exactly go to her, but rather to a single son of her own choosing. And yes, that meant the other sons could end up homeless because of a single decision. Law 153 is, however, a pretty gruesome record of how female murderers were treated. A woman who had killed her husband for another man would end up impaled on a stake; what's more, her lover was also to receive this same punishment as an accomplice. Murder is a heinous crime, but impalement as punishment only comes up this one time in the entire Code (if we exclude the 40 or so laws the stele doesn't have and whose contents are unknown). This crime must have been significant to the judges of Babylon considering how uniquely it was dealt with.

Next came incest and how the law treated it. And judging by the following five laws, it was an offense punishable more severely than today. For instance, law 154 states that a man who sleeps with his daughter should be exiled from the city. The following law speaks of a father defiling his son's wife after the two had already had sex. The father's punishment was binding and subsequent drowning. Next comes law 156, where it deals with the father defiling a virgin before his son had any chance of bedding her. He was to pay her half of a gold mina and compensate her for the dowry she brought. After this, she was free to marry a different man. Law 157 very harshly states that anyone who sleeps with his mother after she had slept with her husband, i.e., the father of the perpetrator, is to be burned alive alongside the mother. The final law of this section, law 158, deals with fathers catching their sons having sex with their main wives, the ones that had children. The son who had committed the act must be exiled from the house.

So, we have exile, drowning, monetary and material compensation, and burning. Interestingly, law 156 specifically references the corruption of marriage by means of incest. In essence, this is actually two laws being broken rather than one, yet the punishment—that of compensation—is far lighter than that of the following law, where both participants of incest end up in flames. But then again, the victim (the wife of the man's son) is technically not family by blood, so the incest in this case is purely one of "spirit," so to speak.

Most of the laws that included marriage up to this point had dowry mentioned in some fashion. The three laws that come next deal with what the future husband and his potential father-in-law arrange prior to the marriage itself. Namely, if the man were to refuse marriage because of a different woman, the father got double the agreed-upon sum for the gifts the man brought (159); consequently, if the father refused his daughter's hand to the man despite the agreement, he paid double the amount of the gifts back to the man (160). The last in the line of these laws is a bit odd, since it includes "slander by a friend" and has the bizarre line "the man's friend cannot have the woman as his wife." The gist of this is that the father still cannot refuse to give away his daughter despite what the man's friend said to them.

Eight laws of this section, 162 to 169, are about inheritance. They are very thorough and detailed, letting the Mesopotamian family know who gets what in case of estate division. According to law 162, if a woman gave birth to sons and died, they were the ones who inherited her dowry (from the time she married her husband), not the father. The following law deals with a woman who bore the man no sons. In case the father of the late wife returned the marriage settlement to the husband (which the husband had to provide before the marriage), then her father was entitled to her dowry, not the husband. However, according to the following law, should the father not have enough to pay for the settlement, this amount was subtracted from the dowry. What remained of the dowry then belonged to the father of the late wife. The next law, 165, deals with the father's death and his inheritance. Usually, a father would choose a "favored son," i.e., the one who would inherit the family name. This son could get a present from his father, such as a garden, a field, a deed, or a house. In case of the father's death, this son got his promised share first. The rest of the estate was then equally divided among all sons, him very much included. Minor sons and their wives are addressed in law 166. In case this son found no wife when the father died, the brothers set aside a little money as a marriage settlement in order to secure a wife for him. Naturally, they split the rest equally. Now, most of these laws deal with a parent dying and the children splitting the estate. But what happens if a father dies, but has children with two wives? Law 167 states clearly that it was the sons who divide up the dowries but only of their respective mothers. The father's estate was divided equally among every individual son, irrespective of who his mother was. The last two laws, 168 and 169, deal with a father wanting to disinherit a son. The first of these laws states that the son could not be disinherited if it could not be proven that he had broken any major law. However, law 169—surprisingly—doesn't immediately leave the son without any inheritance just because of a committed crime. The father was obliged to forgive his son the first time. Yet, if the son committed a crime again, the disinheritance had to happen.

In short, a father had no claim of the land the mother had as her dowry, and it could only go to either her offspring or her own father, depending on the situation. The sons also had to settle who got what from their father while he was still alive before they moved on to any kind of land division. Wifeless sons were to be helped out, in a sense, during the inheritance process, and sons from other mothers were to inherit the dowry first, and then divide the rest of the estate equally with their half-brothers.

The final two laws of this section deal with exclusion and disavowal. In both of them, the son had a chance of having his innocence defended, highlighting the strength of the concept "innocent until proven guilty." Interestingly enough, the latter of the two laws provides room for the son to repent and get a second chance, a rare occurrence in Hammurabi's Code and a welcome addition to it, considering the severity of other penalties for crimes that were either harsher or lighter than this one.

Children were also covered by the law, especially children of slaves and concubines. A man could have children with maids and slave women, but if he were to acknowledge them as his own during his life, they also got part of his estate after his death (170). If the opposite were true, the maid and her children were set free, and the wife remained on the estate which she could use, but not sell due to her children inheriting it (171). But it's law 172 that somewhat complicates the whole matter—if the wife had no dowry, she was to receive a portion of the land equal to that of one of the sons, but if the children were to conspire against her and it was proven that she was innocent, she was to remain in the house. And, on top of that, if she chose to leave, she had to leave what her husband had gifted her during marriage and gain a new dowry from her father as she prepared to be remarried. It's amusing to see all of this additional info crammed into a single law like this, considering it looks more like several laws bundled together.

Yet this string of laws doesn't end there! That same woman could have children with her new husband, and once she died, both her old and new children divided her dowry amongst themselves (173); if she had died before giving birth again, the dowry belonged to her sons from her prior marriage (174).

Law 175 departs from this and deals with slaves fathering children with women of higher status. The children could not be claimed by the slave's master, as they were free citizens. Slaves, however, still had some difficulties in this legal area; 176 stipulates that a slave could take a wife from a higher status and that the two could work together to earn more property, but after his death, his land was to be divided equally between the wife and the master. In short, if your parent was a slave, you could only hope to inherit half of what he had prior to dying.

Wives and widows are one thing, but priestesses and remarried women are another, and the eight laws that follow cover their place in Babylonian law. Remarriage had to take into account the prior estate, the children, and the reselling of property (or rather, a ban thereof). A widow that still had children who were minors couldn't remarry until a judge looked over her specific case, according to law 177. The judge was obliged to look into the state of her first house. If all was in order, this house fell under the management of the second husband and the widow herself. They had to legally officiate this decision with a document. Within this house, she had to take care of her children and maintain it without selling anything. Should someone buy the goods from her house, they lost the money immediately, and the utensils went back to the widow's house.

Then come the laws regarding the priestesses. Law 178 stipulates that a priestess or a devotee could gain a portion of her father's inheritance from her brothers that inherited it, and if they failed to do so, she was to have the land herself. Naturally, she was not to sell the land. The next law in line directly links to this one and states that if the father of the priestess specifically claimed that she can do whatever she wanted with her property, then the brothers got nothing.

180 makes it clear that the daughter gained the amount of produce or grain after the father's death if he gave her this as a present, while the rest of the estate went under the ownership of her brothers. However, according to 181, a temple maid or virgin without such a present got only a third of her potential inheritance. A slight difference appears with the priestesses of Marduk, the titular deity of Babylon; these priestesses got a third of the house which she could use, but not sell. After her death, this part of the estate went to whomsoever she wanted it to go to (182).

Concubines would not be treated as well as wives in terms of property; a father could give a concubine a dowry upon marriage, but she received nothing from his estate after he died (183). In case she got nothing during her father's lifetime, the brother who inherited the wealth provided the dowry and attempted to secure a husband for the concubine (184).

Ten laws close this subsection, and they deal with a very peculiar topic for the ancient world, that of child adoption. One look at all ten of these laws paints a picture of both the benefits and flaws of being adopted. First, there's law 185, which stipulates that once a man adopted a son and raised him as his own, the biological father could not claim him as his own son (should he change his mind about the boy, of course). Then there's law 186 that states a punishment for the adopted son if he hurt his foster parents. By this law, he was to return to his biological father, presumably losing all rights he might have had as the son of a new family. Sons of prostitutes or temple devotees were also unable to return to their biological parents, according to 187. The same goes for artisan parents and their adopted children, as the following law stipulates. However, there's an addition to this law in the form of law 189, wherein an adopted son might not have learned the craft and had to be returned to his original parents. The son could also return, as law 190 states, if the foster father didn't rear him equally with his other children. Law 191 then deals with inheritance. An adopted child could be disinherited in favor of the biological children of the adoptive father. However, the adopted son couldn't just be abandoned by his father; the father had to provide him with a third of the inheritance his biological children would get. This did not include the field, the garden, or the house. The last three laws, namely 192, 193, and 194, again show us how cruel Babylonians could be with punishments. Sons of temple maidens or prostitutes were forbidden from rejecting their adoptive parents, and if they did, their tongues were cut off (192). Eyes were plucked out of any prostitute's or temple maid's son that claimed the house of his biological father while rejecting his foster parents (193), whereas a nurse that had to take care of a newborn child but instead nursed a different one while the original child died would lose her breasts for lying to the parents (194).

Adopted children were not to be returned unless something extreme, like neglect of a child or assaulting the original parents, were to happen. The social class of the adopter also dictated where the adopted child remained. Artisans could keep their new "apprentices" if they taught them what to do, and children of prostitutes or temple personnel no longer belonged to the original parents. Adopted children also had the ability to be compensated should the father have the idea of disavowing them, but any unseemly behavior on their side was very brutally punished (for example, cutting off the tongue or pulling out an eye).

The entire section dealing with assault basically contains only one subsection, or twenty laws. Most of them are essentially the same principle told in a different way, but as an example of what this principle was, only two laws are really needed for an explanation:

196. If a man put out the eye of another man, his eye shall be put out.

200. If a man knock out the teeth of his equal, his teeth shall be knocked out.

One of the laws most often compared to the Hammurabi Code is biblical law. The reason for this lies in these two particular laws, which can best be summed up with the famous quote "An eye for an eye, a tooth for a tooth." A consensus between historians is that most nations in the region, Jews included, had a set of common laws which they codified (separately from one another) and presided over in courts. Most of the principles of these ancient nations match each other, so much so that it's nearly impossible to talk about Hammurabi without mentioning the Hebrew Bible.

However, assault wasn't judged, tried, and punished the same due to different social strata. Slaves were often punished more severely (205), whereas free men paid differently from men who were just freed from slavery (203, 204), and hitting someone of a higher status would bring about a penalty of public whipping (202). Striking a man without intent would result in paying their medical bills (206) or compensation if the struck man died (207). Women are covered in the final six laws of this section. Any man that struck a free woman and caused her to lose a child she was carrying had to pay ten shekels for compensation (209). In more drastic cases, if that same woman died alongside the unborn child, the daughter of the man who hit her was also to be killed (210). However, women of the lower class would only get five shekels for the loss of their unborn child from the man who hit them (211), and half a mina went to her family if she died from that blow (212). Maidservants were on an even lower scale, as they would get no more than two shekels for that same exact crime (213), and their families only received a single third of a mina in case of the woman's death (214).

Yet again, we see that women were protected by the law, but it was important to be born in the right class, much like with the men charged with assault. Women of all social layers are covered here, and other than 210, all of them specify monetary compensation rather than capital punishment.

The section regarding the fees for different professions is, admittedly, a bit more tedious than the earlier ones, but it gives us a decent insight into how professionals were treated in Hammurabi's Babylon. Eleven laws cover how much doctors and vets were paid, depending on the class of the customer (215, 216, 217, 221, 222, 223, 224) or how they were penalized if they made a mistake (218, 219, 220, 225). What follows are two laws regarding barbers who accidentally removed slave marks. Law 226 states that a barber that cut off the slave sign of a person that wasn't sold yet would lose both of his hands. On the other hand, a barber could be tricked into doing this. The person who tricked the barber into this action was sentenced to death and post-death burning in their own house. The barber only had to swear that he didn't do it consciously and he was free of any guilt (227).

The oath-swearing in 227 is more of an afterthought than a condition, considering it follows the pretty well-thought up penalty for the man who tricked the barber into messing with the slave's sign.

The remaining 13 laws here deal with boatmen and builders, and follow roughly the same formula as the laws before them. Of these, only three deal with how much the craftsman was to be paid (228, 234, 239), with literally all the other laws in this subsection dealing with punishments. The most brutal are the ones dealing with accidentally killing the owner of the house or his family members (229, 230). All other laws in this group stipulate compensation in terms of money or goods.

Nearing the end of the stele, three more sections make up the remaining 41 laws. Agriculture comes first, and the first ten laws of the subsection talk about cattle, specifically oxen. Any ox impressed for forced labor was worth a third of a mina (241), whereas a year of using or "renting" plow-oxen could cost the tiller up to four gur of grain (242). Renting herding cattle would cost a Babylonian three gur of grain (243), a gur less than those of an ox for plowing. Then there was the issue of losing animals. Lions could kill oxen or asses in the field, and their loss was on the owner of the animals, not the person renting them (244). Each ox that the tiller would harm or kill had to be replaced and be compensated for to the owner (245), and the same applied for broken legs or cut neck ligaments of bulls (246) and pulled-out eyes, which only earned half of the bull's value (247). The fractions continue in law 248, where a broken horn, a snipped tail, or an injured muzzle could only get the owner of the harmed bull a fourth of its value in compensations. Yet there were times when the gods above would "smite" the bull, at which point the tiller merely had to swear an oath that this had happened, and he would be guilt-free (249). He would also be innocent if a random stranger were to push the ox in a crowded street and injure it (250). What's more, the owner would have to compensate others if his ox was proven to be one that was prone to injuring others (251); in that case, he had to clip his horns or fasten it, but if a man was murdered by this ox due to the owner's neglect of the animal's violence, the owner had to pay half a mina of money to his family. This money was reduced to a third of a mina if the bull killed a slave (252).

It's important to state that none of these laws contains capital punishment. In other words, harming an ox or being harmed by one was never dealt with death, but rather exclusively with repaying the owner or the victim. Naturally, it goes without saying that the status of the owner of the victim will influence the gravity of the penalty.

The next four laws touch upon cattle but specifically deal with embezzling goods. Stealing the grain from the original owner while working on his field would result in the hired thief losing his fingers

(253), whereas not tending to the field (254) and subletting the yoke to someone else and keeping the grain (255) only demanded material compensation. Law 256 is interesting considering how "creative" its punishment is: the embezzler was to plow the field by force ("be left on it with the cattle," as the law states) if he was unable to repay the amount the previous law states he must provide.

The eleven laws that close this subsection up talk about the hiring of individuals and the laws pertaining to them. Of these, one is sadly incomplete (law 262), but it clearly refers to cattle and is more than likely linked to the law that follows it. The laws cover prices for the services of field laborers, herdsmen, and ox-drivers (at the time a separate job title from, say, someone herding sheep) paid in grain (257, 258, 261), as well as compensation in case something was stolen or ruined during their services (259, 260, 263, 264, 265, 266, 267). Of these, only 266 deals with the potential innocence of a herdsman if something happened to the herd; once more, we see the oath sworn before the gods used as a "get out of jail free card," though the circumstances for when it could be used were very specific, e.g., if a god or a lion kills an animal.

The last two sections all consist of one subsection each. Laws 268-277 all more or less serve as a continuation of the previous subsection, as they deal with hiring rates for beasts of burden, workers, and vehicles. Of these, the first three are exclusive to animals. 268 states that twenty ka of grain was the price for an ox used to thresh. The next law cites the same price for threshing, but this time the animal is an ass. Young animals of any kind were priced at ten ka (270).

What follows are prices of hiring wagons, with or without a driver and an ox. According to 271, an ox, a cart, and a driver would cost 180 ka of grain for a single day. However, 272 lets us know that just the cart was worth forty ka of grain, also per day.

Human workers weren't left out of this either. Law 273 states that a laborer hired to work from April to August (naturally, the law is represented in Babylonian months; this is a rough estimate of the time converted into the units we use today) was to be paid six gerahs of money for a day's work. From August to the end of the Babylonian year, the price would go down to five gerahs. Law 274 is a bit fragmented, but it deals with hiring artisans (potters, tailors, ropemakers, masons, etc.). Sadly, not all prices are available, but they fluctuate around five gerahs per day, some going up or down a gerah or two.

The hiring of ships and boats was also included in the code. Ferryboats would cost three gerahs of money per day to rent (275) and freight boats two and a half gerahs (276). Were Babylonians to rent a ship and pay sixty gur for it (277), one-sixth of that money would be paid up front as the rent money for the same day the boat was rented.

A gerah, at least according to the Bible, roughly amounted to 0.60 grams, or 0.02 ounces, whereas a gur amounted to 303 liters, or 80 US gallons. However, different sources cite different amounts for these ancient units of measurement, but these numbers are the most accurate close estimates.

Five laws round up the code portion of Hammurabi's Code, and they deal with slaves. Law 278 deals with slaves as "defective goods"—a slave that caught a specific disease was to be returned for a full refund, regardless of the slave's gender. Sometimes a third party would claim slaves that someone had already purchased, and law 279 states that the original owner of the slaves has to deal with this claim. Laws 280 and 281 are the last pair of laws in this Code to be closely conjoined, and they deal with slaves taken from a different city. If their previous owner recognizes them and they're all from the same city, they go to him without the new owner getting his money back; if they are from a different city, the new owner was to swear their price before the gods, get said money, and then relinquish the slaves to the service of their old master. The final law, 282, deals with punishment of a male slave who declares that his owner isn't his master. The appropriate punishment of an ear being cut off is implemented here, as slaves, while in service of their masters, had to know their place. Of course, this law stipulates that the master had to prove that he owned the slave, but sadly we don't know what happens if he was proven wrong since this is where the law section ends.

A cylinder seal worshiping the sun-god Shamash[ix]

The Epilogue

As can be expected, the epilogue contains a lot of self-aggrandizing by Hammurabi. Once more, he restates how he subjugated the north and the south, how he brought peace to the land of Sumer and Akkad, and how he maintained balance and harmony within the borders of his empire. But it's what comes next that really gives historians a clue as to the purpose of the stele with these laws:

The king who ruleth among the kings of the cities am I. My words are well considered; there is no wisdom like unto mine. By the command of Shamash, the great judge of heaven and earth, let righteousness go forth in the land: by the order of Marduk, my lord, let no destruction befall my monument. In E-Sagil, which I love, let my name be ever repeated; let the oppressed, who has a case at law, come and stand before this my image as king of righteousness; let him read the inscription, and understand my precious words: the inscription will explain his case to him; he will find out what is just, and his heart will be glad, so that he will say:

"Hammurabi is a ruler, who is as a father to his subjects, who holds the words of Marduk in reverence, who has achieved conquest for Marduk over the north and south, who rejoices the heart of Marduk, his lord, who has bestowed benefits for ever and ever on his subjects, and has established order in the land."

When he reads the record, let him pray with full heart to Marduk, my lord, and Zarpanit, my lady; and then shall the protecting deities and the gods, who frequent E-Sagil, graciously grant the desires daily presented before Marduk, my lord, and Zarpanit, my lady.

This is Hammurabi directly talking to his subjects, to the people who will benefit (or be affected) by most by the laws listed here. Hammurabi was a king who cared for his subjects, or rather this is the impression he wanted to leave, and as such providing them with the means of achieving justice was not only expected but almost obligatory. Yet, it's not only the people Hammurabi commissioned this Code for, as the epilogue continues:

In future time, through all coming generations, let the king, who may be in the land, observe the words of righteousness which I have written on my monument; let him not alter the law of the land which I have given, the edicts which I have enacted; my monument let him not mar. If such a ruler have wisdom, and be able to keep his land in order, he shall observe the words which I have written in this inscription; the rule, statute, and law of the land which I have given; the decisions which I have made will this inscription show him; let him rule his subjects accordingly, speak justice to them, give right decisions, root out the miscreants and criminals from this land, and grant prosperity to his subjects.

Much like later rulers and diplomats (Constantine VII Porphyrogennetos, Niccolò Machiavelli), Hammurabi composed this work for the future ruler of his land, stressing how important it was to rule justly and fairly. He specifically noted, later in the epilogue, that any king who followed this Code to the letter should receive the blessings of the gods, and that any ruler who tried to change, erase, or destroy the code (which indeed happened later) should be cursed by those selfsame gods. The majority of the epilogue goes, in quite substantial detail, over all the different curses each god or goddess shall bring about to anyone sacrilegious enough to defile this monument.

Notes on the Code; Common Misconceptions

Since its appearance, Hammurabi's Code was the subject of fierce debate even when it came to some basic questions, such as its intended purpose and makeup. With almost a century and a half of archeological and historical research, there are only a few details which the experts can ascertain about this magnificent monument.

The first and possibly most important question that needed to be answered was the purpose of the Code. Contrary to popular belief, and even contrary to the very name of this stele, Hammurabi's Code is not really a code. It wasn't used in judicial disputes, and references to the laws it covers are very few and far between, and even those are more conjecture than anything. In other words, judges did not use this stele as a reference point when they presided over legal cases. People involved in research regarding this Babylonian ruler have been wondering for years what reason this "code" was really created for if not for codifying the law of Hammurabi's new land. The best we can make out is what the ruler himself stated in the epilogue. This law was one of many monuments that glorified Hammurabi during his time, and more than that, it was meant to show everyone, noble and slave alike, how benevolent yet just Hammurabi was. Much like other steles in Mesopotamia during this period in history, it was created to boost the ruler in the eyes of the masses, but in a way that made them feel just as important to the kingdom as he was. Another possible purpose is that the Code is merely a collection of laws based on previous cases that have already been presided over. Convenience, if anything, could have driven the ruler to inscribe them on black diorite, and the message to future rulers regarding maintenance and usage of this Code further strengthens this argument, though not by much. Scientific consensus behind these claims is still not entirely clear, and until more direct evidence comes out, we can only speculate.

Another important detail to note about this Code is that it's by no means exhaustive. At best, it only contains civil laws. There are no references to military law or anything resembling "foreign policy," and there's no doubt that both of these elements had legal regulations attached to them. We don't know what laws there were for conscription, years of service, dealing with POWs, or how treaties were enacted (though some laws tangentially touch on some of these topics), nor do we know how a foreigner was treated if he wanted to live in Babylon, not as a slave or prisoner, but as a free agent willing to buy land or set up shop in the city. We also don't get any laws regarding the health sector (other than a few pertaining to surgeons and veterinarians) or schooling, nor are there any laws dealing with potential emergency events, e.g., wars, natural disasters, famine, an epidemic of a disease. While the Code is pretty expansive in and of itself, it simply doesn't contain many of the elements a codified set of laws should undoubtedly have.

Chapter 7 – Hammurabi's Legacy

There's little doubt that Hammurabi was influential throughout Mesopotamia. If we focus merely on the positive aspects of his domain, we find a plethora of ways in which this Babylonian king managed to change the entire political, religious, and cultural landscape of the entire region between the two rivers.

One thing that Hammurabi was especially proud of was the massive achievements regarding justice. Several poems and hymns committed to steles excavated at Ur and Sippar show how proud he was of his ability to rid his lands of wrongdoers and instill justice and proper law in his lands. He fancied himself a warrior, a peacemaker, and a champion of justice, and with the Code of Law standing tall some century and a half after his death, and now adorning the ever-busy hallways of the Louvre, there's a good argument to be made that he was right.

Hammurabi, of course, didn't really need to brag about his achievements, as others did that for him. In fact, unlike any ruler of his dynasty, he was deified years before he would leave the throne and pass away. The practice of declaring a ruler a god wasn't exactly uncommon in the Ancient Near East, but this was the first time a Babylonian was honored with this act, and it didn't stop there. Hammurabi even lived to see children being named in honor of him, such as Hammurabi-ili, which translates to "Hammurabi is my god."

Oddly enough, he wasn't the first person to be named Hammurabi, as even during his reign there was a ruler of a different city with the same name, as mentioned earlier in this book. The spike in popularity of that name had to come from his long and eventful reign though, and it's no wonder that two more rulers bore that name, both of them members of a different dynasty altogether. Again, this was not an isolated practice—Sargon was equally popular to the point of a much later ruler taking his name, as were other noteworthy kings of any city-state in the region.

Hammurabi was such a notable monarch that even people who lived an entire millennium after him remembered his name. Later poems and stories would evoke his name much in the same way they would with a deity such as Ishtar or Shamash. If we were to use modern terms, we could say that Hammurabi had entered "the mainstream" of Mesopotamia's wider culture. His Code of Laws was a monument to this, and it's no wonder that Shutruk-Nahhunte, an Elamite king, raided Babylon in 1158 BCE and decided to take multiple valuable relics of the past, which included at least three stelae containing the Code. They found their home in Susa, not to be discovered until centuries later by a few curious European researchers. The Code even made its way to Assurbanipal's massive Assyrian library, where it was listed and kept.

The Code itself can be said to have influenced multiple other legal systems of antiquity. Hebrew law, famously, contains references to a few laws listed here, specifically those relating to the "an eye for an eye" principle. Its discovery was so important to worldwide legal heritage that the US capitol's House Chamber received a portrait of Hammurabi in 1949 as one of 23 people who influenced the creation of the American legal system. It's fascinating to think that, while a great fraction of his life was dedicated to conquest and war, Hammurabi is still remembered as an agent of peace and justice. Unlike Sargon, who is remembered for his conquests, or Utu-hengal who liberated the Sumerians from outside influence, or even Gilgamesh whose legendary battles inspired some of the most wonderful works of early fiction, Hammurabi will always be the lawgiver, the peacekeeper, the ruler who actively worked on bringing justice to his people.

Samsu-iluna cone, 1749-1712 BCE, currently in Chicago, IL[x]

Conclusion

Hammurabi was undoubtedly a ruler of vast historical significance. With a reign lasting over four decades, he managed to grow from a local prince who cared more about rebuilding temples and repairing canals to a unifier of numerous kingdoms and a subjugator of former "great powers" of the ancient Middle East, from someone who was subservient to whoever was in charge at the time to a dominant despot whom everyone feared and respected. Like few kings and emperors before him, he had united the region under his foot, but unlike his predecessors, he had changed how countries functioned in Mesopotamia forever. With him, the age of the city-state died, and the first age of empires was born. It's no wonder then that his name rang loud and true centuries, even millennia, after his death.

But he was more than just a powerful conqueror. His relations with conquered cities, while not always great, spoke volumes of how he treated his subjects. At least on the surface level, Hammurabi tried his best to pacify the region, rebuilding local temples and taking the people's livelihoods into account. His now famous Code, more than anything else, shows that justice among his subjects was his principal concern, and for the briefest of times, Mesopotamia enjoyed a unified legal treatment, one where they could rely on their ruler to maintain justly and one where he himself frequently participated in as the supreme judge regardless of how minor the case was.

Finally, his Code more or less changed how we view history, influencing future generations as much as it did past ones. Scientists and scholars are now questioning the age of biblical law, and they sought parallels between this code and many that followed, and, as the research grew, even the laws that preceded it. Mesopotamian history itself is so indebted to Hammurabi that the principal ways of measuring time include the years of his reign as a reference. The adjective "far-reaching" doesn't do this king justice, as his influence goes beyond that.

Ultimately, Hammurabi was human, and though his humanity is visible only in bits and pieces through epistolary communication of his peers, it nevertheless shows us that even the most legendary of warriors, rulers, and leaders had some frailty to them. Examining the Code itself, as well as Hammurabi's actions, lets us know that he wasn't as perfect as he portrayed himself to be (like all rulers of his time did), but these imperfections only make his contribution to world history more powerful. Hammurabi will only continue to fascinate future generations of researchers, and with each year new sources will surface, providing us with more precious information about this spectacular Babylonian king.

Check out more Captivating History books

Free Bonus from Captivating History (Available for a Limited time)

Hi History Lovers!

Now you have a chance to join our exclusive history list so you can get your first history ebook for free as well as discounts and a potential to get more history books for free! Simply visit the link below to join.

Captivatinghistory.com/ebook

Also, make sure to follow us on:

Twitter: @Captivhistory

Facebook: Captivating History:@captivatinghistory

Bibliography

Ancient History Encyclopedia (2009). Retrieved on November 3rd 2018, from https://www.ancient.eu

Duncan, G.S. (1904): The Code of Moses and the Code of Hammurabi, In *The Biblical World* Vol. 23, No. 3, (pp. 188-193). Chicago, IL, USA: The University of Chicago Press

Encyclopaedia Britannica (1981), Retrieved on November 3rd 2018, from https://www.britannica.com/

Gadd, C. J. (1973): Hammurabi and the End of His Dynasty. In Edwards, I.E.S., Gadd, C.J., Hammond, N. G. L., and Sollberger, E. (Eds), *The Cambridge Ancient History* Vol. 2 (pp. 176-227). Cambridge, UK: Cambridge University Press

Gelb, I.J. (1948): A New Clay-Nail of Hammurabi, In *Journal of Near Eastern Studies* Vol. 7, No. 4, (pp. 267-271). Chicago, IL, USA: The University of Chicago Press

Kent, C.F. (1903): The Recently Discovered Civil Code of Hammurabi, In *The Biblical World* Vol. 21, No. 3, (pp. 175-190). Chicago, IL, USA: The University of Chicago Press

King, L. W. (1919): *A History of Babylon.* London, UK: Chatto & Windus

Langdon, S. (1920): The Sumerian Law Code Compared with the Code of Hammurabi. In *The Journal of the Royal Asiatic Society of Great Britain and Ireland* No. 4, (pp. 489-515). Cambridge, UK: Cambridge University Press

Luckenbill, D. D. (1917): The Name Hammurabi. In *Journal of the American Oriental Society* Vol. 37, (pp. 250-253). Ann Arbor, MI, USA: American Oriental Society

Lyon, D. G. (1904): Notes on the Hammurabi Monument. In *Journal of the American Oriental Society* Vol. 25, (pp. 266-278). Ann Arbor, MI, USA: American Oriental Society

McNeil, D. G. (1967): The Code of Hammurabi. In *American Bar Association Journal* Vol. 53, No. 5, (pp. 444-446). Chicago, IL, USA: American Bar Association

Neugebauer, O. (1941): The Chronology of the Hammurabi Age. In *Journal of the American Oriental Society* Vol. 61, No. 1 (pp. 58-61). Ann Arbor, MI, USA: American Oriental Society

Orlin, L. L. (2007): *Life and Thought in Ancient Near East*. Ann Arbor, MI, USA: University of Michigan Press

Price, I.M. (1904): The Stele of Hammurabi, In *The Biblical World* Vol. 24, No. 6, (pp. 468-472). Chicago, IL, USA: The University of Chicago Press

Prince, J. D. (1910): The Name Hammurabi. In *Journal of Biblical Literature* Vol. 29, No. 1 (pp. 21-23). Atlanta, GA, USA: The Society of Biblical Literature

Rutz, M. and Michalowski, P. (2016): The Flooding of Ešnunna, the fall of Mari: Hammurabi's Deeds in Babylonian Literature and History. In *Journal of Cuneiform Studies* Vol. 68, (pp. 15-43). Alexandria, VA, USA: The American Schools of Oriental Research

Slanski, K.E. (2012): The Law of Hammurabi and Its Audience, In *Yale Journal of Law & the Humanities* Vol. 24, No. 1, (pp. 97-110). New Haven, CT, USA: Yale University Press

The Avalon Project (2008), Retrieved on November 3rd 2018, from http://avalon.law.yale.edu/ancient/hamframe.asp

Thompson, R.C. (1928): The Golden Age of Hammurabi. In Bury, J.B., Cook, S.A., and Adcock, F. E. (Eds), *The Cambridge Ancient History* Vol. 1 (pp. 494-551). Cambridge, UK: Cambridge University Press

Van de Mieroop, M. (2005): *King Hammurabi of Babylon.* Malden, MA, USA: Blackwell Publishing

Vincent, G.E. (1904): The Laws of Hammurabi, In *American Journal of Sociology* Vol. 9, No. 6, (pp. 737-754). Chicago, IL, USA: The University of Chicago Press

Wikipedia (January 15, 2001), Retrieved on November 3rd, from https://www.wikipedia.org/

Notes on Images

[i] Original image uploaded by Dbachman on 28 July 2005. Retrieved from https://commons.wikimedia.org/ on November 2018 under the following license: *Creative Commons Attribution-ShareAlike 3.0 Unported.* This license lets others remix, tweak, and build upon your work even for commercial reasons, as long as they credit you and license their new creations under the identical terms.

[ii] Original image uploaded by Daderot on 9 June 2015. Retrieved from https://commons.wikimedia.org/ on November 2018 under the following license: under the following license: *Creative Commons CC0 1.0 Universal Public Domain Dedication.* You can copy, modify, distribute and perform the work, even for commercial purposes, all without asking permission.

[iii] Original image uploaded by Marie-Lan Nguyen on 21 February 2009. Retrieved from https://commons.wikimedia.org/ on November 2018 under the following license: *Creative Commons Attribution 2.5 Generic.* This license lets others remix, tweak, and build upon your work even for commercial reasons, as long as they credit you and license their new creations under the identical terms.

[iv] Original image uploaded by Heretiq on 4 August 2005. Retrieved from https://commons.wikimedia.org/ on November 2018 under the

following license: *Creative Commons Attribution 2.5 Generic*. This license lets others remix, tweak, and build upon your work even for commercial reasons, as long as they credit you and license their new creations under the identical terms.

[v] Original image by MapMaster. Uploaded by Thamis, published on 26 April 2012 and retrieved from **www.ancient.eu** on November 2018 under the following license: Creative Commons: Attribution-ShareAlike. This license lets others remix, tweak, and build upon your work even for commercial reasons, as long as they credit you and license their new creations under the identical terms. Please note that content linked from this page may have different licensing terms.

[vi] Original image uploaded by Marie-Lan Nguyen on 11 December 2012. Retrieved from https://commons.wikimedia.org/ on November 2018 under the following license: *Creative Commons Attribution 2.5 Generic*. This license lets others remix, tweak, and build upon your work even for commercial reasons, as long as they credit you and license their new creations under the identical terms.

[vii] Original image uploaded by Chad and Steph on 17 October 2010. Retrieved from https://commons.wikimedia.org/ on November 2018 under the following license: *Creative Commons Attribution 2.0 Generic*. This license lets others remix, tweak, and build upon your work even for commercial reasons, as long as they credit you and license their new creations under the identical terms.

[viii] Original image uploaded by Osama Shukir Muhammed Amin on 24 April 2018. Retrieved from https://commons.wikimedia.org/ on November 2018 under the following license: Creative Commons Attribution-Share Alike 4.0 International. This license lets others remix, tweak, and build upon your work even for commercial reasons, as long as they credit you and license their new creations under the identical terms.

[ix] Original image uploaded by Marie'Lan Nguyen on 2 February 2006. Retrieved from https://commons.wikimedia.org/ on November 2018 under the following license: *Public Domain*. This item is in the

public domain, and can be used, copied, and modified without any restrictions.

[x] Original image uploaded by Daderot on 22 August 2014. Retrieved from https://commons.wikimedia.org/ on November 2018 under the following license: under the following license: *Creative Commons CC0 1.0 Universal Public Domain Dedication.* You can copy, modify, distribute and perform the work, even for commercial purposes, all without asking permission.

Printed in Dunstable, United Kingdom